My Language Is a Jealous Lover

Titles in the **Other Voices of Italy** series:

## Other Voices of Italy: Italian and Transnational Texts in Translation

Editors: Alessandro Vettori, Sandra Waters, and Eilis Kierans

This series presents texts of any genre originally written in Italian with the aim of introducing new or past authors, who have until now been marginalized, to an English-speaking readership. It also highlights contemporary transnational authors as well as writers who have never been translated or who were translated in the past but need a new translation. The series focuses on the translator as a crucial figure for the dissemination of art and knowledge, increasing the appreciation of translation as an art form that enhances cultural diversity.

This book addresses several of these goals and thus it is an ideal text to include in this series. It was written by an exophonic, transnational author of Italian descent who moved from his native Argentina to Italy at the age of twenty-four. Fittingly, he works as a librarian and is constantly surrounded by books. The main subject of *My Language Is a Jealous Lover* is language itself: how it shapes people, and how people transform and utilize it. It introspectively explores issues of communication, memory, and experience—what is lost and gained in switching languages. The book delves into how language can both alienate and unite its users, as well as the reasons why writers leave behind their first language to write in another. The author includes plentiful anecdotes from his life that mirror the experience of other exophonic writers such as Nabokov, Beckett, and Joyce, who also write in a language they acquired as adults. The translators, scholars of Italian in constant transition between languages, have faithfully brought the author's love of languages to the forefront of the book.

# My Language Is a Jealous Lover

ADRIÁN N. BRAVI

Translated by Victoria Offredi Poletto
and Giovanna Bellesia Contuzzi

Rutgers University Press
New Brunswick, Camden, and Newark, New Jersey
London and Oxford, UK

Rutgers University Press is a department of Rutgers, The State University of New Jersey, one of the leading public research universities in the nation. By publishing worldwide, it furthers the University's mission of dedication to excellence in teaching, scholarship, research, and clinical care.

Library of Congress Cataloging-in-Publication Data

Names: Bravi, Adrián N., 1963– author. | Bellesia Contuzzi, Giovanna, translator. | Poletto, Victoria Offredi, translator.
Title: My language is a jealous lover / Adrián N. Bravi ; translated by Victoria Offredi Poletto and Giovanna Bellesia Contuzzi.
Other titles: Gelosia delle lingue. English
Description: New Brunswick : Rutgers University Press, [2023] | Series: Other voices of Italy | Includes bibliographical references and index.
Identifiers: LCCN 2022010610 | ISBN 9781978834583 (paperback ; alk. paper) | ISBN 9781978834590 (hardback ; alk. paper) | ISBN 9781978834606 (epub) | ISBN 9781978834613 (mobi) | ISBN 9781978834620 (pdf)
Subjects: LCSH: Second language acquisition—Psychological aspects. | Authorship—Psychological aspects. | Bilingual authors—Language.
Classification: LCC P118.2 .B72713 2023 | DDC 401/.93—dc23/eng/20220524
LC record available at https://lccn.loc.gov/2022010610

A British Cataloging-in-Publication record for this book is available from the British Library.

References to internet websites (URLs) were accurate at the time of writing. Neither the author nor Rutgers University Press is responsible for URLs that may have expired or changed since the manuscript was prepared.

www.rutgersuniversitypress.org

He spoke Russian in fifteen languages.
—Julia Kristeva

# Contents

# Translators' Note

*Some Challenges in Translating*
*Exophonic Authors*

The Italian publisher has defined this book as "a series of short chapters somewhere between autobiography and essay in which Italian-Argentinian writer Adrián N. Bravi explores what happens within himself and within other writers who decide to abandon their mother tongue in order to write in another language." Bravi's text resonated profoundly for its translators, who grew up bilingual in the UK and Italy and have now been living in the United States for over forty years. The book was a true labor of love. We were deeply aware of the irony of a pair of exophonic translators ferrying the work of an Italian-Argentinian into American English.

Bravi states that the writings of exophonic authors prove that languages are living things in constant exchange, traveling from one point to another: "they migrate, go into exile, they translate themselves, they define new ways of thinking and seeing." Research on bilingual brains confirms that when a bilingual person hears words in one language, the other language is also activated. As translators we were faced with an Italian text infused with Bravi's native Argentinian-Spanish concepts, allusions, and references whose essence we strived to maintain in English.

Another challenge was the translation of the numerous quotations included in the original text. They fell into three categories: some were Italian translations of English texts that needed to be found and reported in their original language; others—for which we followed the same procedure, while resisting the temptation to edit them—were Italian translations from other languages or original Italian texts that had already been translated and published in English. Finally, for those quotations that had never been previously published in English, we provided our own translation.

With regard to the title, we thank our editors for suggesting "My Language Is a Jealous Lover," which instantly captures the very essence of Bravi's reflections on language. In the body of the text, however, we opted to translate "gelosia" with "possessiveness" rather than "jealousy," which in English, we felt, would not be imbued with the same powerful sense of possessiveness that the Italian implies. We are thankful for the constant support of Adrián Bravi, who was always ready to explain ambiguous points in his narrative. His co-operation was invaluable.

In conclusion, we felt strongly about bringing this work to the English-speaking public. We are thankful to the *Other Voices of Italy* editors at Rutgers University for choosing this text as one of their very first publications. It reflects the intense interest in the transnational, translingual, and transcultural approach that is pervading the study of the humanities and, in particular, of languages today.

Victoria Offredi Poletto and
Giovanna Bellesia Contuzzi
Smith College, Northampton, MA, July 2022

# Foreword

## *Living and Writing between and across Multiple Languages*

I am grateful to the editors of *Other Voices of Italy* for inviting me to write a foreword to this book. I have channeled my observations into a dialogue between my experience and that of the author, focusing on key themes that resonate with me: memory, language, migration, and translation. Reading Bravi's book awakened old memories that sparked an introspective journey of self-consciousness. My experiences, ideas, and reflections point to how we as human beings have more in common than what separates us. We create the "Other," the one who does not look like us or speak like us. Today we mostly call that other "the immigrant." I began by reading a few chapters in the Italian version of *La gelosia delle lingue*. That language has been familiar to me since childhood. Pages were scrolling on my desktop. Each chapter made my emotions whirl, a kaleidoscope of powerful images. Images that spoke the language of family, home, travel, love, joy, and at times pain and bitterness. Reading between Bravi's episodes from his own life as well as his references to famous exophonic writers, I connected with them first of all in relation to the vast theme of "language." The stories of writers who for various reasons left their country and adopted another language made me reflect on how I could identify with the ideas they were expressing. I was listening closely to what they were saying. In some passages I could hear my own story: switching languages, abandoning my mother tongue, exile.

Bravi was born in Argentina and is of Italian descent. He emigrated to Italy when he was twenty-four years old. I was born in Mogadishu-Somalia. My mother was Somali and my father was a Pakistani born in Zanzibar with a long history of family migration. I left my country and came to Italy when I was eighteen. Bravi and I are two different people, who come from two different continents. In these troubled times, where more and more people are crossing borders and switching languages; where racism, hatred, and nationalism are on the rise, reading his work makes me realize that Bravi's thoughts, his research, his personal story are both unique and universal. Everyone will find that he speaks to them.

In the opening chapter "Childhood," Bravi writes about how his life has changed. He spent the first half of his life thinking in his first language, and the second half in another language: Italian. A language that does not have a past for him. Castilian is the language of his childhood, a language frozen in time; it does not get old. He reflects on words like *lagartijia*, *crecida*, *barro*, and *camalotes*. These words are so powerful and his memories so vivid. He recounts his childhood playing with cousins and friends, toying with a lizard. He is sitting on top of the kitchen table in his old house by the river, watching his parents while they are busy cleaning the floor from the water that flooded it. Every one of these words when translated into Italian lacks the loving cocoon of his childhood. While I was reading this passage, my father came to mind. He was in his thirties when he settled in

Somalia from Kenya. In childhood, he spoke Urdu with his family. English was part of his school curriculum, and Swahili was the language spoken in his hometown. Starting a new life in Mogadishu he had to learn Italian, a language that followed him through to his old age. Dad was busy trying to improve and perfect this new language and was fascinated by its musicality. He spent the last sixteen years in Italy, where he passed away. He never spoke in Urdu to me except for humming a lullaby. Now that I am older, I wish he had taught me his mother tongue. I feel as if a part of my heritage is missing. I could learn Urdu, but it makes no sense for me now. That language will never be soaked with childhood memories.

The voices of migrants from various parts of the world converge in these chapters of Bravi's book—their difficult choices, the resilience, the sacrifice, the success they build. The story of Bravi's aunt where she tells of her dramatic journey across the Atlantic just after World War II is particularly touching. It reminds us of the millions of Italians who have emigrated to Argentina since 1871 in search of a better future. Sadly, we tend to forget our history, and we lack empathy toward the other people who come knocking at our shores. They are young men, and women carrying their infants. They are refugees fleeing from war, persecution, dictatorships—discriminated against for religious, ethnic, or political reasons. And migrants leave their countries because of poverty, climate change, and dead-end futures. They travel packed into small rubber boats, risking their lives to reach Europe, the land of safety and opportunities. We listen to the news of people drowning in the Mediterranean without being indignant; it becomes the norm. They are numbers without a history, a name, and politicians continue to alarm us by describing them as invaders. People who come to steal our jobs and threaten our culture. In the last decade, thousands of human beings have lost their lives crossing the Mediterranean Sea. We do not have the exact numbers. They vanish. In "Displacements," Bravi writes: "For some, returning to those places [they left] is sadder than departure was." Unfortunately, this is a tragic reality for many immigrants. I have heard so many stories from friends of the Somali diaspora who went back to Mogadishu after an absence of more than twenty years. For them the return was traumatic: destroyed neighborhoods, their houses occupied, an unrecognizable city. The civil war left many scars.

I share the same opinion when Bravi relates: "Language is always welcoming, open to all arrivals. It does not tolerate walls of division; it does not belong to one group or another. It belongs to all those who speak it, read it and write it, no matter where they come from."

More than one million children who were born in Italy or came to it when they were very young are still considered immigrants and are labeled *stranieri*. Most of them speak hesitantly, if at all, the language of their parents. Italian is their language. Italy is their home, yet they are denied citizenship. The strong, bitter words writer Ágota Kristóf uses when she refers to French as her "enemy language"—a language imposed on her by chance, a language that killed her native Hungarian—shifted my thoughts to the brutality of centuries of colonialism and its consequences. The European colonizers imposed their language and their cultural domination onto the natives. Until recently, in many African countries English, French, and Portuguese were recognized as official languages. Language is power, and, in fact, after thirty years of absence, Italy is planning to return to Somalia through language. The Italian language has been broadcast on Radio Muqdisho since January 2022. Only my generation speaks Italian; some Italian-speaking Somalis have passed away while many others have settled abroad. The young ones speak English and Arabic. What opportunities does learning Italian give them in a world where English is widely spoken? Is Italian my colonial language? Yes, to give a straight answer. Somalia was an Italian colony that became independent in 1960. Somali was an oral language until the development of the Somali script in 1973, when it became the official language of administration and education. Bravi at one point in the book talks about the maternal and the paternal languages. Is Italian my enemy language? Absolutely not. Born into a family that mixed cultures and languages, my parents spoke Italian among themselves. Their choice was a sensible one, as they considered Italian a lingua franca. For me, Italian is not only part of my school curriculum. It is also the language of love, which my family borrowed to transmit to me their values, traditions, culture, and religion. My father played with me, hugged me, and told me stories of his island in a language that did not belong to him. He immersed himself in the world around him, a place where Italian was predominant; at work, in shops and restaurants, at the movies where we often went to watch the latest films, even American ones that were dubbed into Italian. The daily newspaper *Il Corriere della Somalia*, the news broadcast over the radio, and the conversations he had with his friends were in *italiano*. With my mother it was a different story since she nursed me and spoke to me in *Af Soomaaliga*. I am stuck in those voices. They are engraved in my memory; that language flows through me. I can see myself playing *garaangar* with friends. I hear the voice of my grandmother telling me fairytales of Arawelo the Somali queen. I smell the strong aroma of the *heel, dhego yare, iyo qorfe* (cardamon, cloves, and cinnamon) lingering in the air as the kettle boils. I can taste the *bariis iskukaris* (Somali-style rice) that mom cooks. The many boisterous aunties who came to our house at all hours, the neighborhood gossip and jokes. The chatty voices of the people at the market selling chickens and sweet pulpy mangoes. I felt a deep emotional connection with my mom when I spoke Somali. It was our language: *hooyo* (mom) and me, the complicity that united us when we didn't want to be understood by dad. We took our language with us when we moved to Novara, and we spoke it surrounded by crowds of people who did not know where we came from. Since she passed away, I cling to it, keeping it vibrant after decades of my absence from Somalia. Settling in Birmingham, UK, was a blessing: to meet and mingle in the large Somali community and celebrate festivities, wedding parties, graduations, and all the other ceremonies that unite us. I visit the areas in Small Heath where the mini markets and restaurants are located. The warm welcome I receive in a place where everybody speaks my hometown language, and where the items sold are our traditional clothes, the scent of *uunsi* (perfume), the chatting of women shopping around me. It is everything that feeds my energy. Technology makes it easy to converse and laugh in *Af Soomaaliga* with my childhoods friends who live in Toronto, Muqdisho, Bursa, London, Buffalo, and many other cities. We grieve and share bad news in our language. The many Somali satellite channels that broadcast news, talk shows, and music keep me updated on what is happening in Somalia.

I found the chapter "Prisoners of Our Own Language," with its biblical story, particularly interesting: "When a fleeing Ephraimite asked to be let through, the Gileadites asked him: 'Are you an Ephraimite?' If he answered no, the Gileadites asked him to pronounce the word *shibboleth*, chosen as a means to verify his identity." This takes me back to half a century ago. When my family and I arrived in Novara, people used to look at us with curiosity. We were the only family in the city with a dark complexion. Fortunately, I did not have the problem of learning a new language. My teachers since nursery and elementary school were nuns from the Piedmont region. Learning Italian at an early age from native speakers gave me that natural fluidity. But soon I realized that people were focusing on my brown skin, and this made them ignore the fact that I was speaking Italian very well. When I was at the market, or in a shop, or if I asked a passerby for directions, the person would look at me and start to articulate words using verbs in the infinitive tense and a loud voice. I was confused; I could not understand what was going on. I thought some of them had not been to school and had problems using the verbs correctly. In time, I realized that cinema, jokes, and colonial caricatures had made them believe that Africans were unable to speak and pronounce Italian well. In the chapter "The Abandonment of Language" Bravi talks about the Tlingit community in southeast Alaska in which parents refuse to teach their own language to their children for fear that it might stigmatize them. This made me reflect on the opposite problem we have in our Somali communities. The majority of those who left Mogadishu as refugees in 1991, soon after the civil war erupted, were scattered across Europe, the United States, and Australia. They had to adapt and learn a new language, and at the same time they did not want their children to lose their language. The Somali language is called *Afkaa Hooyo*—mother tongue in Somali. The identity of Somalis is linguistic and has a rich tradition of oral poetic literature mainly due to the largely pastoral lifestyle. Nowadays, to prevent it from being lost, it is digitized. Somalis of the second and third generations of the diaspora are born abroad. Many parents are frustrated because their kids are not able to speak the language properly. The problem is that, from preschool to college, they spend all day speaking whichever language is dominant in the host country. At home among siblings, that is the language they use. Parents are worried they will not be able to speak with their grandparents and relatives who are back home. Families try to build close communities where other Somalis congregate, so children can learn their culture and traditions. I have been asked: Why do Somalis group together? People do not understand that it was not a choice for them to leave their country. It was the war that forced them. Adults still dream of returning home. Some believe that their children will want to go back, but this is not the reality. Fortunately, starting in the past few years more families who can afford a trip to Somalia take their offspring there for vacations. Online courses, children's storybooks, and television programs are all tools used to teach the language. The first time I saw the animated cartoon Tom and Jerry speaking Somali I was positively surprised. And I had a real laugh.

In his book Bravi talks about translation and self-translation. I would like to share my experience of these too. When I left Mogadishu in 1971, Somali was not a written language. The Somali that I learned as a child was still an oral language. The official Somali Latin alphabet used today was adopted in 1972, when I had already left the country. In that sense, my primary written language and the language of my books is Italian. However, my childhood memories are "stored" in the Somali language, so I often use Somali words to capture the richness and texture of those experiences. When, for family reasons, I moved to Birmingham, I felt welcomed into that multicultural city. I love going to cultural events, meeting people from different ethnic groups, making friends with locals, discovering the different accents in the English language. I soon realized that living in a place where all voices speak English, nobody, including people in the Somali diaspora, would value my work unless it was translated. Translation came out of the necessity of reclaiming my voice. Initially, I was not confident about translating my own work at all, but the cost of having it translated was prohibitive, so I decided to do it by myself. It was also a way for me to survive, adapt, and eventually to test my voice within a new context. Being the author and self-translating my own work gave me the freedom to write almost a new text. It took some time for me to discover the richness of the culture and the beauty of the English language. That discovery eventually led me to write poems in English. However, the process is never easy because one language almost never translates directly into another. For example, my poem "Wings" was originally written in English and was then translated into Italian as "Ali Spezzate" (Broken wings). I have been asked by students and translators why I changed it. The only reason is that in Italian I needed to express the feeling of being broken, while yearning for freedom. But in English, the noun "wings" itself felt sufficient to convey this meaning.

I would like to conclude these notes, inspired by Bravi's book, with a question about translation. I have been puzzled: Why is that when I search for "Mogadishu" in English on Google the images of the past civil war, of its horror, come up? And why, when I type "Muqdisho" in the Somali language into Google, all the beautiful images of today's city appear: the Lido beach with crowds of families enjoying themselves, boys playing football, the city rebuilt, streets full of life?

Shirin Ramzanali Fazel, novelist and poet

My Language Is a Jealous Lover

# Introduction

In 1983, on the tenth anniversary of the death of W. H. Auden, Joseph Brodsky wrote *To Please a Shadow*, a memorial tribute in English that also serves as his position statement on the act of switching languages:

> When a writer resorts to a language other than his mother tongue, he does so either out of necessity, like Conrad, or because of burning ambition, like Nabokov, or for the sake of greater estrangement, like Beckett. Belonging to a different league, in the summer of 1977, in New York, after living in this country for five years, I purchased in a small typewriter shop on Sixth Avenue a portable Lettera 22 and set out to write (essays, translations, occasionally a poem) in English for a reason that had very little to do with the above. My sole purpose then, as it is now, was to find myself in closer proximity to the man whom I considered the greatest mind of the 20th Century: Wystan Hugh Auden.[1]

There are many reasons why someone might abandon what the Ancient Romans called the *materna lingua*. If for Brodsky, choosing to write in English was the best way to get closer to W. H. Auden, for Beckett choosing to write in French was his way of coming to terms with the musicality of language. Other authors, instead, experienced their exile and the resulting encounter with another country, as a constraint. This happened to the writer Ágota Kristóf, for instance, who considered her host language, French, an enemy language that had erased the Hungarian of her childhood. This also happened, in part, to the Romanian-French philosopher and essayist Emil Cioran who thought that switching languages was a catastrophic event in the life of an author. It also happened to Brodsky himself, who, conversely, denounced his mother tongue, Russian, as a symbol of corruption, complicit with totalitarianism.

Switching from one language to another means running a risk. It is not always a successful undertaking. It is not a matter of being at ease with or having command of a language, but rather of being a part of it, living it, and transforming it from within. Every encounter we have with a language, be it a foreign or our native one, presumes a *rebirth* and a point of no return. We do not speak this language or that language: we exist in different languages. We see, we observe, we listen and we love through a language. A language that is our eyes and our very essence.

Memory itself is a form of language: we never remember something in the same way in two different languages. Changing language involves, in some way, reprogramming ourselves. Our life is somehow rewritten, reinterpreted in the light of a new experience. It is a gradual process. Rewriting also involves the act of scraping away. We write and, at the same time, we cover up. It is an experience of death and rebirth, that requires no scribe, no creator. Each of us experiments with different registers and with different ways of reinterpreting our own lives.

Migration itself should be examined from a linguistic point of view, because that is precisely where one's *identity* and memory reside. Childhood voices are the only homeland of the migrant or the person living in exile. We might build ourselves a new life, in another country, but our memories and our past will remain locked within those voices.

This book was born, on the one hand, from my need to address the hospitality offered by a language, hospitality that I always found among the pages of Italian authors, among dialects and regional idioms. On the other, it is a way for me to understand certain authors who for various reasons have switched languages or who have analyzed the process of doing so. I have tried to re-examine some linguistic structures, to ask myself at each point in this puzzle, what happens within us when we have to come to terms with a language other than our own. Switching languages involves distancing, inner distancing that sometimes even manages to split one's own story. Walter Benjamin wrote: "Traces of the storyteller cling to the story the way the handprints of the potter cling to the clay vessel."[2] Those handprints, I like to think, are the perfect metaphor for the relationship that each one of us establishes with their own language: the one in which they have chosen to live, to breathe, and to experience the world.

# ~ 1 ~

# Childhood

My life is almost exactly split in half by a sort of linguistic watershed. I spent the first half speaking and thinking in one language and the second half in another. I would have never imagined that my first language, Spanish, or more precisely Castilian, which I used until I was about twenty-four, would become a mutilated language for me. A language without old age, while Italian has no past for me, no youth, because the colors and flavors of my childhood speak another language. For me it is not the same thing to say *lagartija* (lizard) or use its Italian equivalent, *lucertola*. It is the same little critter, but in my imagination, they are two different creatures. The word *lagartija* takes me back to the first half of my life, when I, along with my friends and cousins, chased these very fast critters, and some of us (not me, I never summoned up enough courage) managed to catch one and pull off its tail. So, the word *lagartija* also conjures up our astonishment at how the torn off tail continued to wriggle while the lizard escaped behind a bush. And all of us, friends and cousins would say: "Mirá, mirá cómo se mueve" (Look, look how it wriggles). The Italian word *lucertola* is devoid of this legacy of memories and excited looks.

The same thing happens to me, more or less, when I think of the Italian word *inondazione* (flooding). In my family we did not use the similar-sounding term *inundación*, but rather *crecida* or *riada*, actually, more often *crecida* than *riada* (which was a word that seemed to belong to the past, an archaic term). The Italian word *inondazione* reminds me of more recent disasters; *crecida* instead, takes me back to my childhood and to my first memories of the time when I lived in San Fernando in an old house by the river. When the *crecida* arrived, my mother would put me on top of the kitchen table and leave me there while she, along with my father and the rest of the family, worked hard to contain the water that came from the river. On second thought, that table was, and still is, my real country. Especially right now, if asked to identify my real homeland, I would say it is that table. I drew my first pictures and perhaps my first letters on that kitchen wall covered by a thin layer of crusted mud left behind by the receding waters. After one of my parents put me on that table, I spat on my finger and used it to scratch the mud. The *crecida* was also surrounded by other words connected to that world. Even though these words remained in the background, they were part of our collective imagination: *barro* (mud), *camalotes* (sort of floating islands formed by aquatic plants), *umbral* (door threshold where the water seeped in, which had to be reckoned with every so often). Should the word *crecida* disappear, a whole world attached, or more precisely contained in it, would disappear from my memory as well.

When I was four or five years old, we moved away from that house in the *bajos* of San Fernando, and after that, the word *crecida* almost disappeared from my daily vocabulary. Other words were added though, words such as *trenes* (trains) or *escondida*. "¿Vamos a jugar a la escondida?" "Why don't we play hide-and-seek?" we used to say. That was the time when we moved to Santo Lugares, another area of Buenos Aires, near the railroad, a few yards from the home of the famous novelist Ernesto Sabato. His house had a garden in the front with no iron fence, just a low wall that was easy to climb over. That was my favorite place to play hide-and-seek. The actual house was all the way at the back of the garden, and I rarely made it that far. It was covered in thick green ivy that seemed to cascade from the roof. The garden, instead, was full of trees, wild plants and layers of fallen leaves that had piled up over the years. I remember a tall araucaria, a mulberry tree, a *gomero* (known in English as a rubber tree, a tree that is perfect for climbing) and a few cypresses. I doubt Ernesto Sabato knew of our forays. I spent a good part of my childhood playing and arguing with my friends among those trees, which I remember as impossibly lush, almost part of a fantasy world. Time often warps memory, and so we often recall the places of our childhood through young eyes, a time when dimensions, colors, scents, were different from our current adult perception. That garden is still frozen in time for me; I see it the way I did forty years ago. When I think of it, I feel as if I were entering an enchanted, or almost enchanted, place.

A few months before Ernesto Sabato died, I saw his garden again. I was with my son who was the same age as me when I used to hide among those trees. Just like many other times before, I was tempted to ring the bell, but I did not. Now there was a rather tall iron fence along the sidewalk that blocked all entry. The trees were still there, not as many as

I remembered, but they were there, and so were the fallen leaves scattered on the ground. I tried to reconcile my memory with the garden I was seeing in front of me. It was completely different, as if the garden of my childhood and the current one belonged to different times that had nothing to do with each other. Inside that house, with the facade still covered in ivy, was Ernesto Sabato, a ninety-nine-year-old writer, fighting against time who, from the window of his room, was perhaps also witnessing the disappearance of that garden.

# ~ 2 ~

# Displacements

Those who live far away from the places where they grew up often find themselves recalling the time and places of their childhood. Distance is a thread that ties us to a time that is within us, a time that becomes memory, image, nostalgia. It is not an emotional state locked in the realm of regret, but rather a way to understand the relationship between ourselves and the world. We are always disappointed when we return to places we remember; the new aspect of these places always makes us aware of the passage of time, of a time long gone, of time as an agent of change.

To remember is to bring what is faraway in the past towards the light of the present. For some, returning to those places is sadder than the departure was. We become aware of our estrangement; we feel lost. Yet, memories are the only link we have to the past. In one of his *Letters to a Young Poet*, Rilke imagines being in a prison with very tall walls that let no sounds in and he wonders if, without any perception of the world, we would still have our childhood "that precious, royal richness, that treasure house of memories?"[1] The bodies, the words, the light, the flavors, the shadows, all the components of our memories are part of our language. Memory is a form of fiction. It exists because the past does not continue, and therefore each time we need to reinvent it, assembling the fragments of those lost moments. Our memories create the map of our fantasies. Gaston Bachelard states that "Memory is a field littered with psychological ruins, a bric-a-brac of memories. Our whole childhood is to be reimagined. In doing so, we have the chance to find it again in the very life of our reveries as a solitary child."[2] We live reinventing our existence; we are in fact this invention that we narrate to ourselves.

Several years ago, Antonio Prete published a book titled *Trattato della lontananza* (Treatise on distance) in which he retraces the most important and meaningful types of distance: from final goodbyes to exile, from exile to the poetics of the gaze, from cartography to perspective, from the sound of distance to the love from afar of the medieval troubadours. In this treatise there is a paragraph that addresses the nostalgia for a lost time. It is titled "Un'irrimediabile lontananza: il tempo irreversibile" (An irrecoverable distance: the irreversibility of time); this is how it starts: "In reality, we are not feeling nostalgic for a place, but for the time we spent there. Not for childhood, but for the period of time it encompassed. That time is definitely lost. We will never be able to return to it."[3]

To quote the Italian poet Giacomo Leopardi, no return to "the same house I lived in as a child" can bring back the time lived there. We can move from one point to another in space, but we cannot do so in terms of time. It is only through memories that we are allowed to see ourselves again because our past selves no longer exist. "Once again I see you / But myself, alas, I fail to see" is a line in a 1926 poem about Lisbon written by Alvaro de Campos, one of Fernando Pessoa's heteronyms.[4]

Prete's "insurmountable displacement" entails, on the one hand, the loss of a part of ourselves and, on the other, the loss of the faces, the voices, the atmosphere and the landscape that combined to create our own profile. They are not two different things: we were that landscape, those faces, and those voices were our own. Yet, we always go back, with words and memories to that "house where I lived in as a child," to that language that contains us and of which we are an inseparable part. "Thinking about distance," continues Prete "is like giving shape and rhythm to the invisible, a language to the unattainable" (9).

I would have never imagined that finding myself faraway in another country, with another language and another landscape, some memories would come looking for me, obstinately, like a band of enigmatic followers: the tango I heard more often as a child than as a young man, the flat and infinite landscape, interrupted here and there by a few trees or some horsemen, the Porteño Spanish of Buenos Aires, the books by Roberto Arlt or Ezequiel Martinez Estrada. All part of a world that already existed inside of me, perhaps hidden because it was too close to me. It was only by moving away that it came back into sight. At that point it became doubly real: in the past, and in the present that was rediscovering it, even if in an anachronistic time frame. And when, for instance, I listened to the raspy voice of Adriana Varela or the arpeggios of Atahualpa Yunani, I felt that only distance could bring that world close to me, because that world only existed that way, from faraway, like a simple illusion or a map of my illusions.

# ~ 3 ~

# My Aunt's Languages

I set out from one language and, without meaning to, I landed in another: Italian and Spanish, two similar languages, without clear-cut borders between them. I cannot give an explanation for my departure. I didn't even know how long I would stay away from my country—even today my suitcase is still waiting on top of my wardrobe. What for, I don't know, but it continues to wait. I wanted to get away, to discover a new place, and, if possible, continue with my studies that I had begun in Buenos Aires. In short, I was not leaving for Italy or Europe, I was simply leaving to get away from my country: my desire to leave was stronger than my desire to get somewhere. Mine was not a round-trip ticket, it was definitely just one-way. What drove me was not the desire to take a different direction, to change home or language, I just wanted to leave the leisurely adagio on which

I had built my life. Perhaps my decision sprang from a mixture of naivete and cowardice. Argentina at that time had just come out of four years of dictatorship. Some words that I still had not come to terms with were bouncing around in my head, words that came from that dark period of our history. Not specific voices, but rather a tone, a rhythmic cadence. That uncomfortable sense of belonging that can only come from words that, with the passing of time, begin to weigh on the soul.

Let me give you an example: In *Sud 1982* (South 1982) the third book I wrote in Italian, there is a part about a soldier who returns from the Falklands War. The novel is written along the lines of a possible past, as Ginevra Bompiani defines the past in the works of the writer Antonio Delfini. It is the past seen as a time that could have happened and that perhaps, "had it really taken place, would have had irrevocable consequences for our present."[1] Well, in *Sud 1982* I wrote:

> With the passing of time, I had begun to realize that sooner or later I would leave my country. Perhaps to go to a place where I could think and speak in another language, because where I was I felt like a prisoner of my own words. Everything reminded me of the Falklands: the trenches, the feet caked in mud, the helicopters. My father had warned me: "You should learn a new language from the very beginning, that way you can think and dream without the memory of those old words. New language, new freedom." For the first time ever, I agreed with him.[2]

Now, here in Italy, I feel as though I have regained the paternal language of my family without losing my mother tongue: Argentinian Spanish. So, I speak and write in Italian, but in the background lurks a hidden language that is still suggesting to me words and tones that belong to my childhood. And yet, I feel I do not have a language that is my own; a language free of torments, of insecurities. Wherever I go, I am a foreigner who needs to rummage through words. When I cannot find the right one, I need to sift through chaotic roundabout ways to explain myself. Moreover, Argentinians think I have a typical Italian accent in Spanish while Italians think I have a strong Spanish accent in Italian. Sometimes I feel sad in one language and happy in the other and that way, hopping between languages, my mood changes. Not having been brought up speaking Italian, I rarely feel nostalgic in that language. If, on the other hand, I remember a detail of my childhood in my native language, I feel I am dealing with the world locked inside those words that evoke it.

I do not know if a new language can free us from something, but I do believe it allows us to see the past through different eyes. It allows us to revisit it through a different lens: "You are in your memory" are the words that Edmond Jabès puts in the mouth of a nomad in *The Book of Hospitality*, a memory "which isn't, as could be thought, bound to the past, but chained to the present it makes."[3] Therefore, my memory at a certain point was creating a present full of ghosts and those ghosts, unfortunately, were speaking the language of my childhood.

I had an aunt, one of my father's sisters who, soon after World War II, had left Sambucheto, a village in the Italian province of Macerata, to go to Argentina. She left from the port of Genoa with her four-month-old son and her husband, a Polish man she had met while he was trying to shelter from the German bombs. Their ship had just crossed the Equator, and the supply of drinking water had run out. All the passengers panicked.[4]

My aunt's baby never let go of his mother's breast; perhaps he too was scared. My aunt used to tell us he never let go of her nipple. Other children had attached themselves to her other breast. They wet their lips with the little milk they managed to suckle. Their mothers implored my aunt to help their children. She did what she could with her milk. The children who did not survive were wrapped in white sheets and thrown overboard. My aunt counted five of them and she blamed herself for those five losses for the rest of her life: "Five children that I could not save," she used to say. I never saw my aunt cry when she told this story in Spanish, her adopted language, although she was clearly distraught, even after so many years. But one day, when I heard her tell the story in Italian, for the first time, I saw her cry. That is when I realized that there is an intimate corner in our mind where our past expresses itself in a very specific language. For my aunt it was devastating to recall those moments in her own language. It was the language the mothers were using when they saw their children's bodies thrown overboard, the language in which she had experienced that terrible event. Perhaps memories only speak the language in which they transpired. Having memories speak a different language is like covering them up or making them fade.

Different ways of speaking fragment us, split us apart: "I, who no longer have a language, but am tormented by many, or sometimes, benefit from many, have feelings that change according to the words I use," writes the Argentine author Héctor Bianciotti in his first French novel *Sans la miséricorde du Christ* (Without the mercy of Christ).[5] Therefore, we cannot feel the same sadness in different languages, no more than we can tell the same story in one language or another. We will always feel disconnected, and have a different way of looking at things. Italian, for my aunt, had turned into the theater of an inner conflict, of a journey without return. Looking back on it caused her memories to take on a life of their own.

# ~ 4 ~

# The Maternity of Language I

Is it possible, I wonder, to abandon one's own language, since it is not simply a way of speaking, or better yet, it is not simply a series of grammar rules, but it is, in fact, a point of view? We can, for a variety of reasons, turn our backs on, abandon, or replace our language, but we might never be able to do without the maternity of that language. It remains an irrevocable point of origin, even when we see the world through the lens of a new language. A mother tongue does not simply teach us to speak, it gives us an outlook, a feeling, a point of view on everything. Its syntax is a perspective. We can clothe our life stories in other languages, but the hold that our mother tongue has on us persists because it is a way of being, living and thinking, no matter how we express it. It is a hermeneutic interpretation of the world. We speak our mother tongue in many other languages.

Silvia Baron Supervielle, an Argentine author who also writes in French, has continually reflected on the process of switching languages. In 1998 in Buenos Aires she published a book titled *El cambio de lengua para un escritor* (When a writer changes languages) and in 2007 she wrote *L'alphabet du feu. Petites études sur la langue* (The alphabet of fire: short essays on language) in French. In this book, the Argentinian writer expresses her thinking on the situation: "The more I think about it, the more I feel the first language never dies: it remains silent, but alive, deep in our soul."[1] This means that as we grow up and change language, we carry within us an 'eternal child' whose voice continues to mix with ours and that continues to view things through the eyes of that mother tongue hidden "deep in our soul." It is that silent voice, its timbre obscured by the new language that, at times, continues to talk inside of us. If I consider all these ideas together, I understand what Bachelard writes in *Poetics of Reverie*, "In passing from one language to another, one experiences a femininity, being lost or masked by masculine sounds."[2] It is the mother tongue that uncovers this femininity through the new masculine sounds. Every time we speak, our mother tongue resurfaces in the acquired language.

In Chapter XIII of the first book of his *Convivio*, Dante talks about his love of his mother tongue, which he considers his parents' unifying trait: "This vernacular of mine was what brought my parents together, for they conversed in it, just as it is the fire that prepares the iron for the smith who makes the knife; and so it is evident that it has contributed to my generation, and so was one cause of my being."[3] It is a language that not only represents his parents' union, but also plays a role in his birth, and is, at the same time, the reason for his existence. This maternity of language determines the life and relationship of a child to the world. A native language gives us the eyes through which we continue to view the world, even when we no longer speak it.

Similarly, Italo Calvino, in a bibliographical note placed at the beginning of his *Hermit in Paris: Autobiographical Writings*, writes: "Everything can change, but not the language that we carry inside us, like a world more exclusive and final than one's mother's womb."[4] In my case, I had to come to terms with Italian, a language I have been speaking for over twenty-five years now, albeit still incorrectly at times, and in which I have been writing only for the last thirteen or fourteen years. During my first ten years in Italy, I continued to write in Spanish. I felt too bound to that way of speaking, even if my intention, when I boarded the plane that was taking me to Europe, was to leave my past behind. For ten years I lived an ambiguous and painful relationship with both languages: my language of departure and the one of arrival, my mother tongue and the one I acquired in the country I chose to live in, at least for a while. On the one hand, I clung to my memories, to the words, the metaphors, to the way of speaking of my mother tongue. On the other hand, however, I wanted to free myself from it; not to forget it, but to be able to have my memories speak in a different voice. We live more in a language rather than in a geographical space. I think I understood this when Italian started to become my dominant language.

During a 1987 lecture delivered in Vienna, Brodsky stated that exile is primarily a linguistic event, "For one in our profession, the condition we call exile is, first of all, a linguistic event: an exiled writer is thrust, or retreats, into his mother tongue. From being his, so to speak, sword, it turns into his shield, into his capsule,"[5] a place to find refuge. Consequently, a haven, a place to hide with our memories or our past, to find in that refuge the hidden intimacy of our own language. An intimacy, though, that will never manage to remain hidden like a shuttered space, because in the end we realize that the capsule of our mother tongue was full of windows open to many contaminations.

## ~ 5 ~

# The Language of Love

Author Elias Canetti was born in Bulgaria, in Rustchuk (present-day Ruse), a port city on the right bank of the Danube that had long been attracting people from all over the world. Bulgarians, Turks, Spaniards, Greeks, Albanians, Armenians, Romani, Romanians, and Russians all lived there together. Canetti grew up at number 12 Ulica Slavianska Street in the Spanish Quarter, inhabited by the descendants of the Sephardic Jews who, in 1492, had been forced to leave Spain after the Christian reconquest of the Iberian Peninsula.

From early childhood he was accustomed to moving from language to language. In *Die befreite Zunge* (*The Tongue Set Free*) Canetti himself says that it was quite normal to speak seven or eight different languages, "everyone understood something of each language."[1] Yet, there was one language,

German, "a belated mother tongue, implanted in true pain," that he wasn't supposed to understand (70). It was the language of intimacy, the language of love shared by his parents ("my parents' secret language"). In fact, in Vienna, where they were both studying and first met, they spoke German: "When my father came home from the store he would instantly talk to my mother. They were very much in love at that time and had their own language that I didn't understand: they spoke German, the language of their happy school days in Vienna" (23).

His parents had fallen in love speaking German and continued to express their love in that same language. They recalled the shows at the *Burgtheater* and the dream they shared at that time of becoming actors. German was their language of intimacy and as such, it excluded their son from their conversations, and when they spoke German, Canetti recalled, "they became very lively and merry, and I associated this transformation, which I noted keenly, with the sound of the German language" (23–24). Their everyday language, instead, the one Canetti used with his parents, was the so-called Judeo-Spanish, called Ladino by some in recent times. (It is basically a version of old Spanish from the 1500s with the addition of some Turkish words.) There was also the Bulgarian spoken by the "peasant girls" who worked in the household. They used Bulgarian particularly when they told him tales about werewolves and vampires, "But since I never went to a Bulgarian school, leaving Rustchuk at six years of age, I very soon forgot Bulgarian completely" (10).

When his parents spoke, Canetti used to listen to them and then asked the meaning of certain words. But they just laughed and said that it was too early, that they were talking about things he would only understand when he grew up. At that time, since German was forbidden, he thought his parents were talking about marvelous things that could only be expressed in that language. Sometimes they sang German *lieder*, usually Schubert and Loewe. Then, in 1911 the whole family moved to Manchester in the UK. There, for the first time Canetti's parents translated German for him: "The first German words I mastered came from 'Das Grab auf der Heide' (The grave on the heath)." The song was about a deserter who gets caught and is standing in front of his comrades who are expected to shoot him.

In 1912, when Canetti was seven, his father died. He was only thirty-one-years-old. The following year, his mother and her three children moved to Lausanne to spend the summer months there before moving to Vienna. In Lausanne, the German that the young Canetti studied diligently became the language of love between him and his mother: "Nevertheless, in Lausanne, where I heard French all around me, picking it up casually and without dramatic complications, I was reborn under my mother's influence to the German language, and the spasm of that birth produced the passion tying me to both, the language and my mother" (74).

After her husband's death, Canetti's mother lost those "loving conversations in German," and now she needed to regain the emotional intimacy of that language, "she felt lost without him, and tried as fast as possible to put me in his place" (70).

German was also the language of love for novelist Anita Desai's parents. She was born in India to a Bengali father who had left "the rivers and rice paddies of Bangladesh" to go and study in Germany, and a mother from Berlin. In the Italian introduction to her novel *Baumgartner's Bombay* she writes: "We grew up speaking German since both my parents spoke it to each other: it was a family language, a private secret island in the great sea of Indian languages." At six, Anita Desai spoke Hindi and German, but the first language in which she read and wrote, the language of her future work, was English. When she writes in English, she says: "I found myself suppressing the languages I spoke: Hindi, and German. They always hovered about my tongue even when they remained unspoken. I was always searching for a way to voice them: something deeply central to my being remained hidden, locked up, as long as I did not."[2] *Baumgartner's Bombay* was born of her need to come to terms with these two hidden and locked-up languages: German, her private and silenced mother tongue, and Hindi, representing the author's Indian world. The novel's main character, Hugo Baumgartner—a German Jew who arrived in India and renounced his own language—was also born of this need.

On the topic of the language of affection and love, there is another example I would like to mention. It concerns the upbringing of Héctor Bianciotti, an Argentine author who is a naturalized French citizen. He was born in Argentina in 1930 to Italian parents. Like so many other Italian immigrants who disembarked at the Port of Buenos Aires at that time, Bianciotti's parents had also found learning Spanish difficult, and kept speaking their native Piedmontese dialect with each other. They held back from passing it on to their son for fear it might hinder his learning of Spanish. In an interview he explained, "I spoke Spanish, therefore, but behind it was a forbidden language which my father and mother spoke between themselves, by habit or perhaps to preserve their intimacy."[3]

While Bianciotti's parents recognized the impossibility of making Spanish their own language, their son recognized the impossibility of sharing his parents' language of affection. Bianciotti himself comments on the Piedmontese dialect's many closed sounds and the frequency of the letter *u*, "the twenty-first letter of the alphabet, the letter *u*, that very intimate sound that, not by chance, is part of the word soli-t*u*de" (ibid.). It is worth noting that when Bianciotti first arrived in Paris he felt as though he were chasing after that closed sound, the *u* that represented his lost intimacy with his parents. Later, on other occasions, he revisited the importance of this sound:

> I like to think that in the forbidden language of my childhood, the one my parents spoke between themselves, there was that closed sound of the fifth vowel, that u sound which does not exist in Italian, not in any of its dialects, except in Piedmontese, and which is the *u* of French. A very intimate sound, like a tiny parcel where a part of me had long ago nestled, and which would have caused me to make the voyage unawares, from one language to the other—taking me away from my own in order to deposit me at the edge of another (ibid.).

In 1645 John Milton published *Poems*, a collection that included five sonnets and a *canzone* written in Italian. (A second edition published in 1673 included additional poems, all in English.) Milton considered Italian the language of love and therefore, all six poems are about love. They also reflect the intensity of the experience of writing in another language, a language Milton considered one of the most beautiful. One could say that it is love itself that chooses the language of this brief *Canzoniere* inserted into a collection of English sonnets. It is the language of song and poetry:

Thy praise in verse to British ears unknown,
And Thames exchange for Arno's fair domain;
So Love has will'd.[4]

Choosing the Arno—the river of Florence—instead of the Thames allows Milton to reflect on love and on writing in another language. The literary critic, Furio Brugnolo, in his *La lingua di cui si vanta Amore* (This is the language in which love delights), provides a survey of foreign authors who wrote in Italian. Commenting on Milton's Italian poetry he stated that in Milton's Italian poems, the theme of love "is not only intertwined with his meditation on writing poetry, it is actually dependent on it, on his writing in another language—the language of the woman he loves—which is also the chosen language of love poetry."[5] Love and language seem to be inseparable in these works by Milton. It is indeed love that chooses its language because it can only express itself in the language of Petrarch. With this choice, Milton seems to suggest that the love for poetry can only be expressed through the musicality of Italian, "the language in which Love delights":

They mock my toil—the nymphs and am'rous swains—
And whence this fond attempt to write, they cry,
Love-songs in language that thou little know'st?
How dar'st thou risque to sing these foreign strains?
Say truly. Find'st not oft thy purpose cross'd,
And that thy fairest flow'rs, Here, fade and die?
Then with pretence of admiration high—
Thee other shores expect, and other tides,
Rivers on whose grassy sides
Her deathless laurel-leaf with which to bind

Thy flowing locks, already Fame provides;
Why then this burthen, better far declin'd?
Speak, Canzone! for me.—The Fair One said
    who guides
My willing heart, and all my Fancy's flights,
"This is the language in which Love delights."[6]

# ~ 6 ~

# The Hospitality of Language

I have been writing and speaking Italian for many years, perhaps I even dream in it, I am not sure. I enjoy feeling like a guest in this language that I still cannot master the way I would like to. From the very beginning, I felt welcomed, like a valued guest. Language is always welcoming, open to all arrivals. It does not tolerate walls of division; it does not belong to one group or another. It belongs to all those who speak it, read and write it, no matter where they come from. It takes no account of our origins. It is the first safe haven for a foreigner, a kind of passageway to cross. A passageway with no doors, no barriers. Beyond it lay a history, a culture, an identity that do not detract anything from the diversity and otherness of those who cross it. Being hospitable means to welcome others, in all their singularity.

In his final book, *The Book of Hospitality*, Jewish-Egyptian writer Edmond Jabès who chose French as his language even before his Parisian exile, dedicated a brief chapter to the hospitality of language. It is a dialogue between a foreigner and a host centered on the importance of the act of welcoming, of accepting the other as one of us, as it is a way of being and living in our world. At one point the host asks the foreigner what his nationality is and he, pointing out that the language that welcomes him always becomes his homeland, answers that he resides in the language they are using to speak to each other in that very moment. As children or adults, we enter this home that welcomes us and during our stay we experience in it our imaginary paths, our projects, when we feel lost. With time we end up discovering it, loving or hating it. We follow its inner movements, its variations. Eventually, we realize that this home has transformed us just as, in a way, we have transformed it. Italian, the language in which I find myself measuring every word, is a flexible language that accepts all suggested variations and contaminations whenever offered.

Therefore, hospitality passes on through words. I want to emphasize the notion of being welcomed, of feeling like a guest in a foreign language. Foreigners bend the language that welcomes them in order to give new breath to their own uprooting. Feeling welcomed creates a doubling effect on the guests who are speaking. On the one hand, this sensation affords them the possibility to distance themselves from the host language; they can view it from the outside, they understand that many words cannot be directly translated, and that many others can open up new linguistic horizons. On the other hand, it is precisely this distance that provides them with the possibility of penetrating the language, maybe coyly, on tiptoe, but still penetrating it, understanding it, and getting lost in it.

Marcel Proust talks about creating a foreign language within one's mother tongue: "Beautiful books are written in a sort of foreign language."[1] Deleuze uses this sentence as an epigraph to his *Essays Critical and Clinical*, and in his conversations with Claire Parnet he specifies: "We must be bilingual even in a single language, we must have a minor language inside our own language, we must create a minor use of our own language. Multilingualism is not merely the property of several systems each of which would be homogeneous in itself: it is primarily the line of flight or of variation which affects each system by stopping it from being homogeneous. Not speaking like an Irishman or a Romanian in a language other than one's own, but on the contrary, speaking in one's own language like a foreigner."[2]

Deleuze insisted on the movement through which we can open a line of flight in our own language, which is similar to what Herman Melville's Bartleby does with his enigmatic "I would prefer not to." He pointed out that Bartleby's frequent repetition of this "negative preference," spoken in "a soft, flat, and patient voice" had the same force, the same role as an "agrammatical formula." Deleuze's deep analysis of Billy Budd's stuttering provided another example of this possible line of flight.[3]

On this topic, my friend Alberto Coppari wrote to me in a letter: "I believe that we start doing something good with words not when we become accomplished writers, when writing well comes naturally, but rather when we begin to feel estranged from our own language. In short, a language becomes our own when we lose it." My friend also pointed me in the direction of a similar quote by Austrian writer Hugo von Hofmannsthal: "True love of language is impossible without the renunciation of language."[4]

# ~ 7 ~

# The Enemy Language

In a short book titled *The Illiterate* published decades after *The Notebook*, *The Proof*, and *The Third Lie: Three Novels*, Ágota Kristóf refers to French as an enemy language, imposed on her by chance, a language that killed her native Hungarian. Kristóf found herself living in a country, Switzerland, without knowing how to read or write the language (a place bereft of words, she writes, almost a desert, hence the title of the book): "I know I will never write French as native French writers do, but I will write it as I am able to, as best I can. I did not choose this language. It was imposed on me by fate, by chance, by circumstance. Writing in French is something I am obliged to do. It is a challenge. The challenge of an illiterate."[1]

In November of 1956 Ágota Kristóf left Hungary just as the Red Army was trying to quell the popular revolt.

Together with her husband and four-month-old daughter she crossed the forest to get to Austria and from there, to Switzerland. She arrived in Neuchâtel, a small town on a lake where she lived until her death. It is said that she never forgave her husband for forcing her to flee. "In the beginning," she says referring to her mother tongue, "there was only one language. Objects, things, feelings, colors, dreams, letters, books, newspapers were this language" (18). That is, nothing but one language, Hungarian, that was her universe, from which she was snatched first by the German of the Nazis and then by the Russian of the liberators who immediately became her oppressors. And then there was French, a language she did not choose, imposed on her by circumstances, that became the language of exile. Kristóf said that she would never be able to speak it correctly, in spite of hearing the sounds in the factory, on the assembly line and writing it at night when she returned from work: "I have spoken French for more than thirty years, I have written in French for twenty years, but I still don't know it. I don't speak it without mistakes, and I can only write it with the help of dictionaries, which I frequently consult. It is for this reason that I also call the French language an enemy language. There is a further reason, the most serious of all: this language is killing my mother tongue" (20).

For me Italian, in comparison, has never been an enemy language and yet, I miss certain Spanish words: for example, *pájaro* (bird), such a sunny and poetic word, it rolls off the tongue so beautifully that you want to say it every time you see a bird. Once, in a short story, I used the adjective *procellose* in Italian to describe *stormy* streets, directly translating from Spanish the simple, familiar *calles procelosas*. Then, a friend of mine, Giuliano Salvecchio, told me that the last person to use the adjective *procellose* in Italian, had been the poet Giacomo Leopardi in 1809 when, at the age of eleven, he translated the *Odes* by Horace. In that instance, I not only discovered the existence of the so-called false friends (very frequent between two languages as similar as Italian and Spanish), but I also learned the importance of the meaning of certain structures, that are not always the same and should not be used in the same way. Italian imposed on me a different register from the one that I used before switching languages. It transformed not only the way I write, but also my perception of the tempo, the rhythm of the syntactical organization of the story. Writing them in Italian I see the stories in different ways. When we change voice, even the words assume another timbre, a new tonality. In short, we become aware, as Deleuze and Guattari write in *Kafka: Towards a Minor Literature* that something that can be said in one language cannot be said in another and that the same story can never belong to two different languages with the same intensity. The most successful stories, in fact, are those that find a rhythm in the language that is capable of narrating them.

# ~ 8 ~

# The Possessiveness
of Languages

In 2010 I received an invitation to participate in a series of meetings at the Italian Cultural Institute in Cordoba, Argentina. I accepted with pleasure without realizing how paradoxical it might be to return to my country, after an absence of twenty-five years, to speak in Italian to an Argentinian audience. While in Cordoba, before each meeting, I constantly thought about the strange quirks of fate and asked myself, "How can I possibly be speaking another language in the country where I was born and lived until the age of twenty-four?"

However, I must admit that I would have found myself in difficulty had they asked me to speak in Spanish. Not because I do not know the language, I still know it well, I think, but because my vocabulary, after so many years of absence from Argentina, is much diminished and I have lost that natural spontaneity typical of someone who speaks it fluently. Addressing this very topic, Silvia Baron Supervielle in the already mentioned *L'Alphabet du feu: petites études sur la langue* bears witness to the difficulty of preserving one's own language intact after having abandoned it in order to adopt another: "Such a realization is painful. Two languages, at the same profound level, cannot coexist in a human being. When one of them goes forward the other regresses,"[1] and bit by bit our vocabulary shrinks. It is a very strange fact, in a certain sense, a dramatic one. So, in that situation I would not have found the right words. Many of the things of which I intended to speak had been conceived in another language, therefore, switching language would have only put me in difficulty and I would have felt embarrassed had I been forced to express the right words in a roundabout way.

At the end of one of the meetings in which I had participated, a gentleman originally from Calabria who had been living in Argentina for many years came up to me. His Italian was rather odd; he spoke it with a distinct accent from Cordoba. He told me that he was forgetting his Italian more and more, and in his opinion, Spanish was a beautiful musical language, but too possessive: a language that destroys everything around it, he added, because it always wants to prevail over the others (like French over Hungarian in the case of Ágota Kristóf). It struck me as a particularly apt metaphor. At that moment, it came to me that it would be a good idea to write a book about the possessiveness of languages. These simple reflections on language arose in some way from the story of that Italian gentleman who spoke with an accent from Cordoba.

## ~ 9 ~

# The Fluidity of Language

Perhaps there are not many people today who read Luigi Meneghello's novel *Libera nos a malo (Deliver Us)* published in 1963, one of the most meaningful works of contemporary Italian literature.[1] More than a confessional autobiography seen through the eyes of a child but filtered through the ironic gaze of an adult, it is a vindication of dialect. In this book, Meneghello succeeds in carrying out an in-depth linguistic study of the historical memory of Malo, a small town in the lowlands of the Veneto, in the province of Vicenza. Resorting to a refined plurilingualism: from dialect, to spoken Italian, to literary Italian, Meneghello manages to transform and change the time of the story in such a way that both the past—and the present that recalls it—"put the world of words out of phase with the world of things" (46).

*Deliver Us* forces us to confront the various layers of language with which we have to come to terms when, after many years, we return to the places of our childhood, a childhood made of words and sounds lost and found again: "A man's personality is made of two strata: on top lie the superficial wounds in Italian, French, Latin, or whatever; down below the older wounds that, healing, made scars of the words in the dialect. Touch one and it sets off a chain reaction, very difficult to explain to someone who has no dialect." (46)

The stories Meneghello recounts in this book, Felli-niesque, fable-like, if only for their grotesque connotation, are above all linguistic memories created by someone who has decided to reclaim the saga of childhood through dialect, but without an exact oral representation. Even though he remained tied to his Venetian roots, immediately after the war Meneghello moved far from his native land, more precisely to England. There he founded and chaired the Department of Italian Studies at the University of Reading until 1980. He wrote about feeling Italian, having no identity issues and never feeling exiled. This *dispatration* (which is also the title of his book from 1993, *Il dispatrio*) never severed his relationship with his land of origin, on the contrary, distance proved to be a salvation with respect to his own idea of language and writing.[2] "Our language was made of overlapping layers; it was a work of intarsia. Besides the broad division between the rural language and that of town, there were many other gradations by neighborhood and by generations. Eccentric demarcation lines divided the various quarters, even the courtyards, the entranceways, the very tables at which we sat down to eat."[3]

Therefore, the site of memory must be sought beneath the arcane words of dialect. And Meneghello, by recovering that language, saves things and along with them saves a past. As if saying that things exist or survive also in the words that define them. Dialect in *Deliver Us* does not serve to describe reality, rather, according to Meneghello, it embodies reality itself: "The dialect word is eternally pegged to reality because the word is the thing itself, perceived even before we begin to reason in another language. This is true above all for the names of things" (46).This statement brings to mind a famous essay by Heidegger, "On the Essence of Language," in which the German philosopher analyzes a poem by Stefan George, "The Word," that ends with this simple and explosive line: "No thing may be where the word does break."[4] Language, in this case the dialect from Malo, is the key to accessing the reality of things.

I have the impression that a similar idea underlies the writing of Dolores Prato, the author of *Giù la piazza non c'è nessuno* (There is nobody in the square). It is a novel that was published in its entirety in 1997, fourteen years after the death of the author, thanks to the efforts of Giorgio Zampa. The novel is a world made up of words retrieved from childhood, "endangered words" around which the author weaves beautiful stories, like the one about the noctule bats which hung in dark corners and she identifies as "little demons:" "I was terrified of noctule bats; my fear partly sprang from their name: it evoked darkness, it evoked night, it evoked silence ruffled by their velvet wings, it evoked the name itself, a bad thing, perhaps even worse because it was a noctule. My book referred to them as bats, instead they were noctules, they only came out to meet the night. My night-time fears were entirely of black velvet, like them."[5]

In *Le ore* (The hours), a novel that like Meneghello's book is full of memories that begin with autobiography and end up telling the story of words, Prato writes: "In the village the universe for me was in eyes and in words. In boarding school being always shut in, the universe of my eyes was limited to the landscape, always the same one, to the corridors, to the dormitories, while the universe of words multiplied."[6]

In Prato's writing there is a kind of lexical search which she pursued for her entire life. It is a dense and transparent journey made up, however, of contrasts, of linguistic dichotomies: the language, the dialect from Macerata that she spoke in her early childhood in the house of her aunts and uncles at Treia, and the language of the Salesian school where she lived after elementary school from the age of ten to nineteen. Prato describes this dichotomy in the second part of *Le ore*, published in 1988 by Scheiwiller: the isolation she experiences, bereft of affection, leads her to give substance to the words, to substitute things with the words themselves. These words do not always become "friends." Often, we notice a painful clash between the language of Prato's childhood and that language devoid of affection that she experiences in the boarding school.

In Meneghello, instead, apart from this lexical journey into dialect, straightforward but at the same time rife with obstacles, there is also an attentive reflection on language. At the beginning of his final author's note in *Deliver Us* he writes: "This book comes from inside a world where the language that is spoken is not written; it is a report from one person from Malo to those Italians interested in hearing it, and it is written, necessarily, in Italian."[7] There is also an excerpt in this story by Meneghello that I like to recall because it deals with hearing one's own language after many years of absence, when we realize that many expressions have changed:

Language moves like a current, and normally its noiseless flow is totally silent, because we are in it. But when some emigrant returns, we can measure the distance from the point where he stepped out and climbed the bank. They come back after ten, after twenty years in Australia or in the Americas where they continued to speak the same dialect that they spoke here with us and which we all spoke; they return and they seem to be people from another town or from another age. Yet it is not their language that has changed; it is ours. It's as if the words too are returning to their homeland, and are met with peculiar feelings, often after some hesitation, sometimes even some embarrassment. (142)

Knowing that there is in language an internal change made up of relationships, comparisons, contaminations, leads me to think that everything changes and that language, while registering the changes in things, changes along with them. Languages are like rivers: all it takes is to go away and return after twenty years "from Australia, from the Americas" to realize that they move "like a current." To conclude this brief chapter on this topic, I would like to quote a letter dated April 2, 1727, from Captain Gulliver to his cousin Richard Sympson:

I hear some of our sea *Yahoos* find fault with my sea-language, as not proper in many parts, nor now in use. I cannot help it. In my first voyages, while I was young, I was instructed by the oldest *mariners*, and learned to speak as they did. But I have since found that the sea *Yahoos* are apt like the land ones, to become new-fangled in their words, which the latter change every year;

insomuch, as I remember upon each return to my own country their old dialect is so altered, that I could hardly understand the new. And I observe, when *any Yahoo* comes from London out of curiosity to visit me at my house, we neither of us are able to deliver our conceptions in a manner intelligible to the other.[8]

## ∼ 10 ∼

# Without Style

In his biography of Samuel Beckett, James Knowlson writes
that the passage from one language to another—in Beckett's
case, from English to French and then vice versa—was a
choice involving a kind of liberation, because it signified an
escape from Joyce's shadow, (*"I vow I will get over J.J. ere I die.
Yessir,"* he writes in a letter from 1932 to Samuel Putnam), but
also from the shadow of his adored, yet hated mother, and
finally from Irish rhetoric itself.[1] There is however, something
I would like to point out regarding the passage from one language to another. Knowlson writes: "It was also easier, Beckett maintained, to write in French without style. He did
not mean by this that his French had no style, but that, by
adopting another language, he gained a greater simplicity
and objectivity. French offered him the freedom to concentrate on a more direct expression of the search for being. . . .

Using French also enabled him to 'cut away the excess, to strip away the color' and to concentrate on the music of the language, its sounds and rhythms" (324).

In order to cut away the excess and concentrate on the rhythms of the language, after World War II, Beckett decided to abandon Joycean aesthetics and switch language in order to concentrate on an aphonic literature of the *unword*: "The more Joyce knew the more he could. He's tending toward omniscience and omnipotence as an artist. I'm working with impotence and ignorance," Beckett said in a 1956 interview with Israel Shenker.[2] It is not a case of stylistic exhibitionism, but rather of tension between word and silence. *Watt*, the last novel he wrote in English, during World War II, but published in 1953, essentially marks the turning point. After this book, Beckett will abandon his mother tongue for French. This not only signifies a passage from one language to another or the use of another, but also a new way of conceiving writing and its inner rhythms. Therefore, it will not be his characters who will babble in French, but Beckett himself. His characters, for their part, will be reduced to voices, echoes, pauses, and silences. In 1937, in a letter to Axel Kaum, Beckett writes:

> It is indeed becoming more and more difficult, even senseless, for me to write an official English. And more and more my own language appears to me like a veil that must be torn apart in order to get at the things (or the Nothingness) behind it. Grammar and style. To me they seem to have become as irrelevant as a Victorian bathing suit. . . . Let us hope the time will come, thank God that in certain circles it has already come, when language is most efficiently used where it is being most efficiently misused. As we cannot eliminate language all at once, we

should at least leave nothing undone that might contribute to its falling into disrepute. To bore one hole after another in it, until what lurks behind it—be it something or nothing—begins to seep through; I cannot imagine a higher goal for a writer today.[3]

If Beckett considered writing in an official English "as irrelevant as a Victorian bathing suit" French, on the other hand, gave him the possibility "to bore one hole after another." For Beckett, writing lies beyond the story, enters into the domain of rhythm and the unsaid, and is a matter of style (or non-style). We could say that it is transformed into a musical entity. The passage from one language to another marks a detachment and at the same time the appropriation of a babbled and contracted language, a language "without style." "With French, Beckett purges the imagination of the material and visceral elements of which it is composed. He seeks an expression that is atonic and aphonic. The new language, learned as an adult, gives him the possibility of building a line of defense against that mass of emotional conflicts, that burden of memories and feelings that the mother tongue delivers to their children."[4]

Once that "burden of memories and feelings" is removed, the aphasia, the nothingness that language conceals, is revealed. Switching languages, therefore, not only represents a new way of participating in writing, but also a stylistic choice regarding literature. We have a style when we are able to babble in our own language or, to quote Deleuze: "[Style] belongs to people of whom you normally say, 'They have no style.'"[5]

Today many best sellers are books that seem to be substitutes for current events, and are written in a standard language that no longer evokes any voice. As a result, the auditory connection between the narrator and the listener is gone; no one seems to be able to babble in their own language anymore. Therefore, in a period in which many best sellers are written in a kind of non-language or flat language that is anesthetized and stateless, the equivalent of non-places, it is disconcerting to hear people talk of style or of "writing without style."

What's more, I find it surprising that a new language could give a writer greater simplicity and objectivity since we presume that these aspects—simplicity and objectivity—belong to a language that we already profoundly know. To write and to have a style are inseparable, even when we try to write without style. To speak of a work without style is an oxymoron. Writing is impossible without a style. We might have an aversion for a certain style of writing, but this would already mean taking a stylistic position. Style is that rhythm of a writer's voice that marks the pace of the story. What is striking is that an author might want to focus on musicality and rhythms by choosing a foreign language.

And yet, that is how it works. When we do not fully know the new language we are adopting, or we only know it slightly, we are able to look at it with different eyes, with a musical gaze, we might almost say. At that point reading aloud is fundamental in order to find the right rhythm, through, and thanks to, its sound. The most beloved texts are always those in which the story finds its voice or those in which the reader is aware that there is a rhythm in the narration. When we find that rhythm, that breath of language, writing goes forward on its own. If we were to compare Ágota Kristóf's style when she writes in Hungarian (repudiated poems that she herself considered too sentimental) to her style revealed by her use of French, we would become aware, as it happened with Beckett, of a different way of conceiving a language. In fact, even Kristóf's characters seem an amalgam of gestures, voices, and different tones.

It's worth noting, however, that Kristóf's French, unlike that of Beckett or Cioran (who adopted French in 1947 while translating Mallarmé into Romanian) or even Kundera's French, was born out of need and deprivation, out of the impossibility of expressing herself in her own language. Therefore, a style forged out of necessity: incisive, dry, syncopated, analyzed, and dissected from the outside, as one can only do with an enemy or alien language. Brodsky says: "Style is not so much the man as the man's nerves, and, on the whole, exile provides one's nerves with fewer irritants than the motherland does."[6]

## ~ 11 ~

# The Scent of the Panther

At the beginning of the *De vulgari eloquentia*—Dante's unfinished treatise on language—written around 1304 during exile and abandoned in the middle of the second book, Dante clearly states the originality of his work and the reasons that led him to want to reflect on the vernacular: "Since I find that no one, before myself, has dealt in any way with the theory of eloquence in the vernacular, and since we can plainly see that such eloquence is necessary to everyone . . . I shall try . . . to say something useful about the language of people who speak the vulgar tongue."[1]

According to the writer and literary critic, Maria Corti, the appeal of this partly rhetorical and partly poetic treatise, written in Latin and addressed to the *doctores illustres* (that is, poets and writers) stems from the fact that it is not directly linked to any specific or previous model. However, it opens up an entirely new field of inquiry aimed at capturing the spirit of his age: "In the *Vita Nuova*, Dante acts as a creator of poems, in the *De vulgari eloquentia* he theorizes on the language of poetry. The entire *De vulgari eloquentia* is a function of this: the Adamic language, the vernaculars of the Italian peninsula, the history of their changes, the notion of grammar."[2] Immediately after his proclamation of originality, Dante moves on to the *subiectum* of the treatise—that is, to the vernacular—which will provide the basis for the art of eloquence: "I call 'vernacular language' that which infants acquire from those around them when they first begin to distinguish sounds; or, to put it more succinctly, I declare that vernacular language is that which we learn without any formal instruction, by imitating our nurses. There also exists another kind of language, a one removed from us, which the Romans called *gramatica* [grammar].[3]

Between these two languages: the vernacular or mother tongue (without rules) and that which is acquired, a secondary kind of language (governed by rules, the only such language taught at that time was Latin), Dante makes a clear distinction, as if they belonged to two different bodies of knowledge, one natural, *noble*, the other acquired, artificial: "Of these two kinds of language, the more noble is the vernacular: first, because it was the language originally used by the human race; second, because the whole world employs it, though with different pronunciations and using different words; and third because it is natural to us, while the other is, in contrast, artificial" (1).

For Dante the discourse on language is also a discourse on the art of using *eloquentia* on the part of poets, guardians of the essence of being Italian. So, the theme of *De vulgari eloquentia* becomes the tale of a search, of a hunt by Dante, who wants to discover the vernacular, the most beautiful and most representative of the Italian peninsula, elevated to the sublime by the power of art:

> Now that we have hunted across the woodlands and pastures of all Italy without finding the panther we are trailing, let us, in the hope of tracking it down, carry out a more closely reasoned investigation, so that, by the assiduous practice of cunning, we can at last entice into our trap this creature whose scent is left everywhere but which is nowhere to be seen. . . . But the most noble actions among those performed by Italians are proper to no one Italian city, but are common to them all; and among these we can now place the use of the vernacular that we were hunting above, which has left its scent in every city but made its home in none. (16)

The scent is that of the fleeing panther, that illustrious, almost nonexistent vernacular, that leaves its scent everywhere, but is found nowhere (in *Physiologus*, a founding text of medieval bestiaries, written between the second and the fifth century C.E. in Alexandria, Egypt, it says that the panther uses its own scent to catch its prey, and that wild beasts follow the scent of its voice). After sifting through all the regions of Italy in search of this illustrious language, and after he had described the characteristics of each of these regions, often caricaturing them, Dante comes to the following conclusion: this illustrious vernacular is like a scent that pervades every region of Italy without finding its true identity in any particular one of them. That is, a vernacular that exists in all its phonetic/geographical variants, whose identity is found in diversity (never identical amongst the different communities that speak it). The hunt, therefore, has not borne any fruit because the illustrious vernacular was not found amongst all the forms of speech and dialects that Dante examined.

The panther, tirelessly hunted, always out of reach, cannot be found in any one specific place because it is everywhere, concealed in local speech, in every word. The vernacular is its scent, just as the essence of the illustrious vernacular is its diversity. Therefore, we could conclude that the Italian language exists within all its variants, in its being Other. It is that same vernacular forest where the prey hides. One possesses Italian if one recognizes its internal differences, like a language that is not exactly one, lacking unity. To learn it is like chasing after the scent of a prey that is almost out of reach. Every foreigner who enters into this language is consequently forced to become a kind of hunter as well. The search for a poetic language has, however, revealed the qualities and the strategies of a sophisticated hunt despite the fact that the hunter has lost his prey. Or, as Giorgio Agamben says in a short essay entitled "The Hunt for Language": "At the origins of the Italian literary tradition, the search for an illustrious poetic language is placed under the disturbing sign of Nimrod and his titanic hunt, almost as if to signify the mortal risk implicit in every search for language that seeks in some way to restore its originary splendor."[4]

In the *Inferno*, Dante punishes Nimrod for having had the misguided thought to build the Tower of Babel, causing forever the loss of meaningful language. Therefore, Nembrotto, as Dante calls him, following the *confusion of languages*, will only be able to babble sounds deprived of any sense. Giorgio Caproni dedicates *Il conte di Kevenhüller*, one of the most fascinating collections of Italian poetry of the twentieth century, to this theme of the hunt, published in 1986, four years before the author's death. The ferocious, hunted beast, hidden "behind the Word," says Caproni, in certain ways recalls the one Dante follows *"across the woodlands and pastures."*

> The nebulous panther (felis nebulosa),
> who attracts
> those who reject her, and erases
> those who challenge her.[5]

In this same collection there is a poem dedicated to Giorgio Agamben that ends with a reference to *De vulgari eloquentia*:

> The place
> is safe from the whisper
> from the fleeing beast, which is always,
> it is said, the word.

The hunt for "the fleeing beast" has established, however, a link between the plurality of the spoken forms of speech described in *De vulgari eloquentia* and the idea of the illustrious vernacular. This is a more dignified and more noble language that Dante finds—not yet well codified—in some of the poets he admires and that he seeks to re-establish. Therefore, the panther he is following is the dream of an Edenic language that heals the post-Babel wound inflicted by the great hunter, Nimrod. But it is this very hunt, across the multiplicity of dialects, forever evolving, that favors the environment for the creation of an illustrious language. It is not a case of hunting down lost models, but of identifying this language amongst the various spoken forms and of capturing it. It will, therefore, be this same fleeing prey that will give rise to the Italian of Dante's poetry, a language that will be amenable to welcoming diversity.

## ~ 12 ~

# Prisoners of Our
# Own Language

Language reveals us, lays us bare before the other. It is the only trait that we cannot negate, precisely because it contains our very being in its voice, in its gaze. We can neither pretend nor negate it. In his book *Writing Degree Zero*, Roland Barthes affirms: "Every man is a prisoner of his language: outside his class, the first word he speaks is a sign which places him as a whole and proclaims his whole personal history. The man is put on show and delivered up by his language."[1]

As I read this passage, the story of the Ephraimites comes to mind as recounted in the Bible's Book of Judges 12, 5–6: the Gileadites had intercepted the Ephraimites trying to cross the Jordan River. When a fleeing Ephraimite asked to be let through, the Gileadites asked him: "Are you an Ephraimite?" If he answered no, the Gileadites asked him to pronounce the word *shibboleth* chosen as a means to verify his identity. The Ephraimite, who had no *sh* sound in his language, pronounced the word with an "s"; he was unmasked as the enemy and slaughtered.

Similarly, during the uprising known as the Sicilian Vespers, there were foreigners who were "delivered up by [their] language." On Easter Monday of the year 1282, at the time of Vespers, after a series of protests on the part of the Sicilians, a French soldier stopped and searched a noblewoman in front of the Church of the Holy Spirit in Palermo. The noblewoman was accompanied by her husband who, outraged by this offensive act, succeeded in seizing the soldier's sword and killed him. From this incident sprang the uprising against the French. That day the people of Palermo began a ruthless hunt for the foreigner. History tells us that to identify the French among the populace, the people of Palermo produced some chickpeas (called *ciciri* in Sicilian) and asked people to pronounce its name which contained sounds alien to the French language. Those unable to pronounce it correctly, were betrayed by their own language, and summarily killed. About four thousand French were slaughtered during that uprising.

## ~ 13 ~

# Two Short Stories

*Landolfi and Kosztolányi*

There is a short story by Tommaso Landolfi published in 1937 titled "Dialogue on the Greater Harmonies" about a character called Y who believes he is learning Persian from an expert in that language. This expert delights in mocking his student by haphazardly inventing words and syntax. At some point, Y realizes that he has learned a language that does not exist. In the following passage, Y explains to the narrator of the story, who is also one of the characters in it: "Well, I must tell you," Y began, "that years ago I dedicated my time to a patient and minute distillation of the elements which compose the work of art. By this path I reached the precise and incontrovertible conclusion that having at his disposal rich and varied expressive means is, for an artist, anything but a favorable circumstance. For instance, it is in my opinion far preferable to write in an imperfectly known language than in one that is absolutely familiar."[1]

The motivating factor behind the idea that it is better to write in a language we do not fully know, would appear to be that "anyone who does not know the right words to indicate objects or feelings, is forced to replace them with circumlocutions, that is with images—with what great advantage to art, I leave it to you to imagine" (30). This seems to be an interesting point of view for those who have to adopt a foreign language. According to Landolfi's character, not knowing the language forces the foreigner to create paraphrases and to expand his writing in search of new images. Therefore, not being completely fluent in the language in which we want to write a story, we writers would be forced to find, on our own, new ways to express our ideas, to weave our own writing around a concept unknown to us or that we cannot grasp, and to create circumlocutions, metaphors, neologisms, and so forth.

By stating it this way, we can already discern Landolfi the Mannerist, obsessed by the insufficiency and opacity of the words, eternally searching for a primal language. Y's story continues as the captain (the one who had taught him that nonexistent language) departs on one of his voyages. In his absence, Y decides to get hold of a copy of the works of a Persian author. To his surprise, Y discovers that he is unable to recognize even a single letter. Stunned by this discovery, he begins to examine grammar books and dictionaries. In the end (says Y to the narrator), "The terrible reality was revealed to me in all its horror: *the captain had not taught me Persian!* No point in telling you with what great anxiety I tried to discover whether his language might be something else— Jakuto, or Hainanese, or Hottentot. I got in touch with the most famous linguists in Europe. Nothing, nothing: such a language did not exist and never had existed" (32).

Y will never even know the name of the language that he has learned and in which he has written three poems, a language that he, and no one else, could know, he being the only one to know and possess it; a language without history, without a past, destined to expire along with the only person who could speak it.

I came across another story in which the problem of language is raised in a similar way to Landolfi's, or at least, so it seems to me, in ways that can be compared to Y's story.

I had been in Italy for only a year, two at the very most, and I did not know Italian very well. One day my friend Alberto Coppari called me up to tell me that he had read a story and wanted to read it to me, too. It was by Hungarian writer Dezső Kosztolányi, taken from his collection *Le mirabolanti avventure di Kornél, Kornél Esti, A Novel* published in 1933 (around 4 years before Landolfi's).[2] If truth be told, the title of this story is rather long and descriptive: "*In Which Kornél Esti Chats in Bulgarian with the Bulgarian Train Guard and Experiences the Sweet Dismay of the Linguistic Chaos of Babel*" (123). It is the story of Kornel who is crossing Bulgaria by train. It is nighttime and he cannot sleep, so he leaves his compartment to stretch his legs in the corridor. At that point the train guard appears carrying a lamp. Kornel, the main character in the story, asks him if he smokes, using the only phrase that he knows in Bulgarian and the only one he is able to articulate very well, almost as if he were a native speaker: "It's characteristic of foreigners always to try and speak the language of the country in which they are traveling, they're too enthusiastic about it, and in no time at all it emerges that they're foreigners. Natives, on the other hand, will just nod and make themselves understood by signs" (125).

The train guard says yes, accepts the cigarette that Kornel offers him and begins to tell him—in Bulgarian—a story of which Kornel is unable to understand a single word. He limits himself to occasionally nodding in assent: "The guard talked and talked. What about? I would have liked to know myself" (127). At a certain point, the guard pulled out from his coat pocket a dirty, faded letter written in Cyrillic script. He placed it in Kornel's hand who pretended to read it and then, behaving as if he knew the language, almost as if he were a fellow countryman of the guard, he repeated neutral phrases, good for any occasion, like *yes, yes* or, *no, no,* or *such is life*. Then, the guard showed him the photo of a dog and a packet with two buttons. In that precise moment, he began to weep, at first holding back his tears and then letting himself go. Kornel embraced him and with a friendly gesture tried to reassure him: "I took a firm grip on the guard's shoulders, to instill some spirit into him, and I shouted into his ear three times, in Bulgarian, 'No, no, no.' Choking back his tears, he stammered another monosyllable, which could have meant 'Thank you for being so kind,' but also, perhaps, 'You revolting phony, you cheating swine'" (63).

This story by Kosztolányi is another good example of how, when unable to understand each other, people can still find a meeting point of reciprocal agreement. Baudelaire comes to mind when he states that "the world goes round only by misunderstanding," that it is precisely thanks to universal misunderstanding that everyone can agree, because, if by chance, we were to understand each other, we would be unable to come to an agreement.

This idea is taken up again by Jankélévitch. "Misunderstanding," writes Jankélévitch, "is not merely a sham: it establishes between human beings a certain level of provisional comprehension that, while never replacing a transparent understanding devoid of all ulterior motives, is however more valuable than open dissent."[3] Both stories, the one by Landolfi and this one by Kosztolányi, share the subject of languages and the inability to understand each other, as well as the problem of misunderstanding and of deception. In fact, Kosztolányi's story ends with an act of deception on the part of Kornel:

> At the last moment, however, I took pity on him. When he had given my bags to the porter and I was getting down, I glanced at him wordlessly as if to say "What you did wasn't nice, but to err is human, and this once I forgive you." And I said in Bulgarian only, "Yes." That word had a magical effect. The guard softened, cheered up, became his old self. A smile of gratitude stole onto his face. He saluted me, standing stiffly at attention. He remained there at the window, rigid with happiness, until the train moved off and he vanished forever from my sight. (130)

Two years after the publication of *Kornél Esti, A Novel*, Kosztolányi published a collection of short stories and essays in which the Hungarian author revisits the topic of the incomprehensibility of language. This time in the character of a foreigner who arrives in a country where no one understands him and where he will eventually die. In one of these essays, he draws an amusing comparison among artificial languages that lack all vitality and are incapable of re-evoking the lullabies that our mothers used to sing to us. Both Landolfi and Kosztolányi are two different writers who were able to write of how we can lose ourselves in language.

## ~ 14 ~

# Two Old Children

I still hold in my mind, as if it were a framed picture, the image of two of my great-uncles meeting again in 1984 in Argentina after seventy years apart. It is difficult for me to conceive that all those years encompassed two world wars, other smaller conflicts, mass migrations, fascism, dictator-ships, the economic boom, even the Russian Revolution. In a word, everything that happened since 1914, the year when Alfredo Bravi, the eldest son of a large Italian family, left to go to Buenos Aires. (I am unaware of the reason for his departure, but it pleases me to think that he left in search of adventure.) Those were the years when a new culture began to flourish in Buenos Aires. The years when Roberto Arlt was writing his wonderful novels and his famous *Aguafuertes porteñas*, articles commenting on the changes that Buenos Aires was undergoing at the time. Or the years when,

Borges began publishing his first books of poetry: *Fervor de Buenos Aires*, *Luna de enfrente*, and when Macedonio Fernández wrote *No toda es vigilia la de los ojos abiertos*, one of the texts that gave rise to the idea that metaphysics is a branch of fantastic literature. The city was beginning to assume that mythical aspect that all Argentinian literature of the early twentieth century would come to attribute to it. Surely this great-uncle of mine knew the Calle Corrientes when it was still a narrow street, and who knows if he danced the tango in *las milongas*—or if he just shut himself up in his Italian immigrant shell.

These two brothers were born in a small country village near Macerata where they lived farming the land. As I already said at the beginning of this story, I am talking about two great-uncles of mine, brothers of my grandfather Nazzareno who died in 1962, ten years after he too had left his homeland with his family to go to Buenos Aires where they lived in a neighborhood near the river and he worked as a ferry operator.

Fortune smiled on them, and in 1984 Alfredo and Antonio met up again in a small house in the suburb of Buenos Aires, called León Suárez, where Alfredo lived. As I mentioned before, seventy years had gone by. By that point, each of them had created his own family and his own world and they faced each other almost as strangers. That day, I remember that someone had helped Alfredo get up from his chair to greet his brother who had come to visit him in Argentina. They embraced, leaving their walking canes on one side and also setting aside anything that might prevent them from reliving the moments of their childhood, the years gone by, hidden in the faded corners of old photographs. Before meeting, they each had imagined the other in their own way

(I am not using the verb *remember* because after seventy years memories become pure fiction).

Their embrace, more than a way of recognizing each other, was a way of repossessing a part of themselves lost in time. Now they spoke different languages, one asked in Italian, the other answered in Spanish because he had forgotten his mother tongue. In the morning, one drank *mate*, the other *espresso*; one loved the life of his neighborhood filled with stories and gossip, the other loved getting up early to walk in the fields. Yet, no matter what, they understood each other, even when they looked at each other without saying a single word. In 1989, Alfredo died in his home in León Suárez. Three years later, Antonio passed on in Sambucheto, a small village halfway between Macerata and Recanati.

## ~ 15 ~

# Poetics of Chaos

Exile and migration presuppose the meeting of languages. The relationship between mother tongue and adopted language permeate the biographies and writings of those who abandon their homelands. We write in one language while thinking in another, or we give voice to our past in a foreign language. For me it was a challenge, for instance, to write a dialogue in Italian between two Argentinian soldiers who were on guard duty before the bombings by the British. I am referring to my novel *Sud 1982* (*South 1982*) in which I tried to give a new voice to a story belonging to a precise linguistic context. These are the paradoxes we face when we switch from one language to another.

In *An Introduction to the Poetics of Diversity*, Édouard Glissant, a francophone writer from Martinique, stresses this aspect of linguistic diversity. Nowadays we speak and write in the presence of many languages (no language, in fact, exists in isolation without relating to others). This does not mean knowing all languages. On the contrary, in the words of Glissant: "I take my own language and I shake it up and shift it around, not into syntheses, but into linguistic openings that enable me to conceive of the relations between languages."[1]

Writing in the presence of all world languages is one of the challenges of Glissant's *Poetics of Relation*. We cannot conceive of a language without taking into account its connections and the relationship it establishes with all the others; that is, we cannot think of it monolingually. Glissant remarks: "Multilingualism does not presuppose the coexistence of languages, nor the knowledge of several languages, but the presence of the world's languages in the practice of one's own" (24). This reminds me of the introduction to the Italian edition of the novel *Baumgartner's Bombay* in which the author, Anita Desai, states: "Although I wrote the novel in English, I was aware of all the other languages submerged inside it."[2] This means plumbing the depths of writing and opening it up to all sorts of possibilities. In contrast, a language cannot be defended from the intrusion of other languages that run through it. This norm would not even be applicable to the speakers of a language (it is not possible to impose a language as a template, or as a set of rules). We cannot even protect it like an endangered species without taking into account its *relations*. (Monolingualism is based on the presupposition that my language is my root and that I am ancestrally tied to a place.)

In *Poetics of Relations* Glissant refers to an aesthetics of creolization (of which the Baroque was a fundamental expression because of its space redundancy and its proliferation that went against the demand for unicity), and he introduces the concept of *chaos-monde* which means being open to every possible contamination. It is not chaos or nothingness devoid of norms. Chaos, posits Glissant, is not chaotic: "Its hidden order does not presuppose hierarchies or pre-cellencies neither of chosen languages nor of prince-nations."[3]

The archipelagic reality in the Caribbean or in the Pacific Ocean, according to Glissant, exemplifies the underlying thought of his *Poetics of Relation*: "What took place in the Caribbean, which could be summed up in the word creolization, approximates the idea of Relation for us as nearly as possible. It is not merely an encounter, a *shock* (in Segalen's sense), a métissage, but a new and original dimension allowing each person to be there and elsewhere, rooted and open, lost in the mountains and free beneath the sea, in harmony and errantry" (34).

The linguistic movement of creolization is not, therefore, an intermediate phase of a series of relations, neither is it the conclusive phase of the process. Creolization presupposes multilingualism, it opens up relations and sparks contaminations. Nowadays our linguistic universe is determined by the complexity of relationships. There are many different variations of English, Spanish, or French, and the intangible unicity of language has basically disappeared.

And yet we might ask ourselves: in what precise moment did the Latin spoken on the streets of ancient Rome turn into the modern language we call Italian? When is a language born, and when does it die? When will Italian cease to exist in its present form? "The Italian language . . . is a complex of languages rather than a single one," wrote the poet Leopardi in his *Zibaldone*.[4] Is there a moment when a language penetrates another and transforms it from within? One thing is certain; no language, not even one that is considered sacred can escape its own demise. Turning to the *Zibaldone* again, Leopardi wrote: "Languages are forever altering, not just slightly, but in such a way that in the end they die. . . . So that it can be said that just as no language has lasted *in perpetuity*, so none ever will" (April 18, 1821) (451–452).

These are the *poetics of chaos*. Therefore, it is migratory flows, invasions, oppositions, and complicities that subvert languages, causing both their decline and their enrichment. Perhaps here lies the secret of a language; it yields to other languages, until it undergoes a transformation and becomes something other than its original self.

# ~ 16 ~

# Exile

All living things exist because they migrate, from swallows to lice, from lice to humans. If people did not move away, they would die. From the point of view of taxonomy, humans should be classified among the migratory species. Living means migrating. The concept of a *foreign land* is not an objective reality, it is simply a mental construct.

Even the country of origin often becomes a *foreign land*, both for those who leave and for those who stay. Our whole society is an interaction among individuals; it is in constant flux. The logic behind social fluidity and chaos helps us make sense of the complexity of reality. According to Nietzsche, man is an uprooted, transient being: "What is great in man is that he is a bridge and not a goal: I love those who do not know how to live except by going under for they are those who go over and across," he writes in his Prologue to *Thus*

*Spoke Zarathustra*. (The original German for "go[ing] over and across" was *Übergang* which also refers to a transition, going beyond, or becoming something other than oneself.)[1]

In the fundamental texts of history, from the Old Testament to the *Odyssey*, from the Chansons de Geste to the *Poem of the Cid*, from the *Divine Comedy* to *Moby-Dick*, literature has always talked about exile, about wanderings and voyages. Had he not been exiled from Troy, Aeneas would not have founded Rome, and Ithaca would not have become Ulysses' longed-for point of return without his ten years of wanderings. Perhaps not even Conrad, the modern precursor of exile literature, could have imagined a character like Marlow, voyaging up the Congo River, immersed in a forest without name and without history.

Even the dead migrate, because sometimes death is not the end of our adventure. When Evita Perón died in 1952, her embalmed body was left on display until the 1955 military coup when her husband went into exile and her body began wandering around the world. At the end of 1974 it was returned to Argentina and found its final resting place in the Recoleta Cemetery in Buenos Aires. Even apparently immovable things migrate. The Holy House of Loreto in 1291 was miraculously carried by angels from Palestine to Dalmatia. Three years later it was moved to Ancona, and finally, a year later, it reached its final destination in Loreto.

Even the myth of Cain and Abel can be read as a form of exile. One brother, we know, was a nomadic shepherd; the other had settled in one place and worked the land. When Cain killed his brother Abel he was, fittingly, chased away: "A restless wanderer shalt thou be on the earth" was God's punishment. All of human history can be seen through this curse—being chased away—"exiled" would not have made sense in a nomadic society like Abel's, but it did as a punishment for Cain who had settled on a plot of land. Cain's fleeing is well represented in an 1880 painting by Fernand Cormon, on display at the Musée d'Orsay. The large painting (33 feet wide) is free of religious undertones. The French painter focuses his attention on Cain's tribe fleeing in the desert and is inspired by the opening lines of "Conscience," a poem by Victor Hugo from *La Légende des siècles* (*The Legend of the Ages*):

> When with his children clothed in animal skins
> Dishevelled, livid, buffeted by the storms
> Cain fled from Jehovah,
> In the fading light, the grim man came
> To the foot of a mountain in a vast plain.[2]

God loves exodus and wanderings. In the Bible salvation is linked to exile and punishment: being banished from the community, losing one's rights and one's tribe to be delivered up to the unknown. We might almost say that exile is so dramatic precisely because it takes us far away from our family tombs. Not everyone can bring back dignity to a condition that was imposed precisely to take it away. When we do not agree with the ideological demands of power, expatriation becomes the first fracture point. There is also a hidden exile, made up of loneliness and marginalization: uprooted exiled people who are not even afforded the chance to repair the fracture that was created between themselves and their homeland because they have also lost the ability to tell their stories. In our eyes they increasingly turn into abstract entities wandering, aimless, along the margins of our same society. They are those lost in the night, exiled, migrants, expatriates, refugees. They wander, and they are never welcomed; they cannot leave their own language behind to come to terms with the new language they encounter. Men, women, children, and whole families are relegated to the margins of society, with no possible point of arrival, or they are simply people for whom arriving means further suffering because they have lost their homeland without acquiring a new one and feel, on their own skin, a double exclusion. A few go back, defeated, some are integrated, others continue to wander around the world acquiring more languages, more cultures, and new perspectives.

Exile always confronts us with loss and with the search for new horizons. Exiled people know that any place in the world, any point of arrival, will always be temporary. It is their condition, a strange and ambivalent condition, like that of the stateless individuals for the ancient Greeks: people disconnected from any political community, a condition that is both neutral and disturbing precisely because they are neither indigenous nor foreign, and yet they demand an identity, a culture. It makes us wonder if it would be possible to build a community of individuals who shun any kind of identity, any sense of belonging, or who demand a plural identity.

In a piece on exile, Palestinian writer Edward Saïd quoted a sentence from *The Didascalicon* by Hugh of St. Victor, a Saxon monk who, in the twelfth century, described a man in exile: "The man who finds his homeland sweet is still a tender beginner; he to whom every soil is as his native one is already strong; but he is perfect to whom the entire world is as a foreign land."[3]

Bulgarian-French literary theorist and historian Tzvetan Todorov takes up this same theme in his epilogue to *The Conquest of America*: "I myself, a Bulgarian living in France, borrow this quotation from Edward Saïd, a Palestinian living in the United States, who himself found it in Erich

Auerbach, a German exiled in Turkey."[4] And I, an Argentine who has been living in Italy for a long time but is still unable to understand the reason for his *dispatriation*, I also take up this sentence, stealing it from Todorov, Saïd, and Auerbach.

At the end of his life Plutarch wrote a letter, *On Exile*, to his young friend Menemachus of Sardis to comfort him about his having been sent into exile and encouraged him not to consider this uprooting as an evil in itself. He quotes an intriguing passage concerning Diogenes the Cynic: To those who said to him "The Sinopians condemned you to banishment from Pontus," Diogenes the Cynic replied: "But I condemned them to stay there, out where meet the shore, the breakers of the inhospitable sea."[5]

This passage by Plutarch reminds me of Argentinian singer-songwriter, Facundo Cabral who, while in exile during the military dictatorship, kept travelling around the world like an aimless wanderer. He almost adopted it as his profession. He lived in a condition of constant nomadism; any place became a departure point to reach a new destination. After the fall of the regime, he returned home and someone asked him, perhaps inappropriately, why he had left. Facundo Cabral smiled and answered: "As Diogenes said, it wasn't me who left, it was you who stayed."

# ～ 17 ～

# Writing in Another Language

In a critical essay on the work of Julio Monteiro Martins titled *Un mare così ampio* (Such an expansive sea) and which, in turn is a detailed reflection on the entire body of migration literature in Italy, Rosanna Morace writes the following on the subject of switching languages: "Therefore, there exists no substitution of one language for another: instead there exist subterranean currents, often subconscious that nourish one another, that fuse and that by forging into one, create the wave that then breaks onto the sand: the only one visible to us but behind which are hidden the deep churnings of the abyss."[1]

When we venture into a new language, we never substitute our own, rather it is our mother tongue that makes its voice heard in the other, transforming the syntax, upending the phonetics, or resetting our imaginary with new stories that come from afar; stories that tell of deserts, of journeys or of mythical odysseys on the high seas. Foreign languages bring with them other ways of seeing, other sonorities, other words that override and insinuate themselves into our old imaginaries or into the host language, in order to tell other stories. They are composed of substrata, of contaminations and of new breath. When we hear them, we are immediately aware of a different syntactical pace. Foreigners who speak it create a rhythm and give life to an imaginary that did not belong to their language of origin nor to the language of the new place, and yet they are part of both. Regarding this movement between a new language and another that is loath to let us go, reminds me of a passage by Raffaele Taddeo in *La lingua strappata* (The ripped-out tongue): "For foreigners who have learned Italian as adults, not in an academic context but out of the necessity to communicate with others and the need to interact with the host country, writing in Italian is always an arduous undertaking. Linguistic structures from their mother tongue continue to intrude and wrap themselves around the new language."[2]

Literature forces us to face the dilemma of *existing between languages*. A characteristic of the modern novel is that of *living in another language*. Writers like Conrad and Nabokov, for instance, are prime practitioners who make us reflect on the problem of bilingualism or multilingualism, that act of moving between different cultures and imaginaries or between the various contaminations. Their writings prove that languages travel from one point to another, they migrate, go into exile, they translate themselves, they define new ways of thinking and seeing; in a word, these writers tell us that languages are living things and that we live among languages.

This fact leads us to redefine the concept of a national literature, to revisit it in the light of an opening up that, far from being paradoxical, goes beyond national borders. The nineteenth and a good part of the twentieth were the centuries that somehow established and defined national borders by putting forward the idea that a history of literature is the history of a nation. However, in the period after the Second World War these borders are redefined, be they geographic or linguistic. It becomes necessary to reformulate the concept of literature and of language as being more accepting of the plurality of voices that come into play. Literature progressively shakes off nationalistic chains. Moreover, it is interesting to see how the places that belonged to a determined linguistic context are revisited and invested with new languages.

W. B. Yeats held that literary translingualism, that is, the case of authors who write in more than one language or in a language different from their mother tongue, is impossible. According to Steven Kellman: "Nobody can write with music and style in a language not learned in childhood, and ever since the language of his thought."[3] This line of thought, says Kellman, is shared by T. S. Eliot who maintained that he knew of no case in which a writer created equally beautiful poems in two languages. These are two possibly valid points of view, even though we need only quote a few names to refute this statement (I'm thinking of two poets closer to us like Wilcock and Brodsky who wrote in languages different from the one learned in childhood).

There remains the fact that today literature can no longer be conceived only within the confines of national borders: there are Italians who write from abroad, as did Luigi Di Ruscio from Norway, or like Marino Magliani from

Holland, or even Italian writers who have emigrated and who write in other languages such as Antonio Dal Masetto who left Italy at age twelve. There are also many foreign writers who adopt Italian as their literary language: they explore an unknown language seeking to give it other rhythms. We are not talking about creating neologisms or of using foreign words in the new language, but of forcing words to accept other meanings.

Rosanna Morace opens up a new way of thinking about Italian literature written by foreigners in her 2012 essay: "La letteratura-mondo italiana" ("Italian world-literature)." She prefers to speak of world literature making an explicit reference both to Glissant's book of essays *Treatise on the Whole World* and to a 2007 collective manifesto *Pour une littérature-monde en français* (For a world literature in French) to which Glissant himself also contributed. "World Literature," writes Rosanna Morace, "moves along a fine line that lies between languages, cultures, stories, imaginaries, traditions and religions; it is therefore intimately marked by hybridization that is reflected in the forms, in the narrating voices."[4] In Italy, literature written by foreigners is a more recent phenomenon compared to other countries and has, moreover, very heterogeneous origins. Until recently, the study of this literature was limited to its biographical aspects, to the problem of integration, as if migration or exile in and of themselves guaranteed an aesthetic autonomy to the writing. In other words, a purely sociological or testimonial interest that came before the literary one. Today, instead, critical attention is directed at its philological, stylistic, and literary merits. Rosanna Morace asks herself: "But what transformations is this linguistic and cultural migration triggering? In what ways does it impinge on our literary traditions and our imaginary, modifying them from within? What are the expressive outcomes and the linguistic innovations that this hybridization produces?" (10) These are all questions that we always ask ourselves when we read an author who was forced to change language.

Consequently, these new Melquíades, with their stories and their languages, shake up the local imaginary transforming it, enriching it with new stories and new words.[5] The wealth of a language lies in its possibilities. Many foreigners, through their writings, question Italian, confronting the language with new rhythms and new babblings. By virtue of their extraterritoriality, their stories are messengers of other worlds that sometimes, paradoxically, do a better job of telling the story of our own world.

# ～ 18 ～

# False Friends

False friends are words or sentences in a language that seem very similar to those in another language, but that have very different meanings and are easily misunderstood by those who speak or hear them. They are a thorn in the side of translators. False friends are more common in languages with the same roots than in unrelated ones. They are particularly frequent between my two languages, Italian and Spanish, which belong to the same linguistic family. They exist in all languages, though. An example is the English *embarrassed* and the Spanish *embarazada* (which means "pregnant") and translated incorrectly can create *embarrassing* situations!

This story of the false friends always reminds me of my maternal grandmother who arrived in Argentina in the late 1940s. She spoke a hybrid language, half Spanish, half Italian dialect from Molise and within the same sentence she threw in words from both languages. This mixed idiom of Italian immigrants in Argentina was called *Cocoliche*. It was a pidgin used in Argentinian popular theater that gave birth to a comic character: Cocoliccio, a caricature of a southern Italian immigrant who was mocked because of the way he spoke.

The name comes from Francesco Cuccoliccio, a laborer from Calabria who, at the end of the nineteenth century, worked in the theater company of José Podestá. He spoke Spanish rather badly, but naively thought he was doing pretty well. Some *Cocoliche* words were borrowed by *Lunfardo*, an argot of the underworld that Borges defined *a language specialized in infamy*. It originated among the lower classes in Buenos Aires and mixed numerous words coming from the different languages of the immigrants. The vocabulary of this argot has contributed to the enrichment of spoken Argentinian Spanish. Tango lyrics, for instance, often use *Lunfardo* terms. So, my grandmother, as I was saying, spoke *Cocoliche*, a language riddled with false friends.

I remember once she gave me some money and after a long, convoluted sentence she said: *mancia*. I thought she had said *mangia* (eat!), I still wonder if she said *mangia*, but it seemed highly unlikely for my grandmother to ask me to eat money, so I thought perhaps she had meant to say the Spanish word *mancha* that in Spanish means *stain*. But there were no stains on that banknote, so I went to find my mother because she always understood right away what my grandmother was saying, and she told me that the money was my *propina*, meaning tip or pocket money in Spanish, but expressed by the Italian word, *mancia*. At other times, my grandmother added the word *loro* in the middle of a sentence, and I always fell into the trap. I thought my grandmother, for some reason, was asking about my pet parrot, Pedrito, because *parrot* in Spanish is *loro*. Instead, she was using *loro* in the sense of the Italian pronoun *they/them*. With time I learned to understand her myself. I no longer got confused when she incorrectly used a false friend like *salir*. So, if she happened to say *salire*, I went upstairs and not out of the door because in Spanish *salir* means "to go out" while it means "to go upstairs" in Italian.

What was really fascinating was that in her neighborhood there were many immigrants who came from different regions of Italy, each speaking their own dialect. It was one misunderstanding after another. Two neighbors might stop talking to each other because one thought the other had said something offensive and so on. I was quite amused by all these false friends, and I must confess, I sometimes even miss them now.

# ~ 19 ~

# Interference

Every language has a set of rules that differentiates it from all others but, at the same time, opens it up to a plurality of contaminations. We are all guests and hosts vis-à-vis a language, precisely because we live in a state of endless migration. There is no limit to how much influence a language can bear; each one lives immersed in a sea of pluralities. Uriel Weinrich in his sociolinguistic classic of 1953, *Languages in Contact: Findings and Problems* discusses interference, that is, the introduction of foreign elements into the domain of language: "Interference arises when a bilingual identifies a phoneme of the secondary system with one in the primary system and, in reproducing it, subjects it to the phonetic rules of the primary language."[1] Therefore, it is not a case of changing language, but of a foreign language interfering internally on another. For example, in Argentina, Italian *interfered* in the formation of *Cocoliche* (some Italianisms were first accepted into *Lunfardo* and then into colloquial Spanish). When I consider these forms of *linguistic interference*, the 1906 book by Roberto J. Payró, *The Marriage of Laucha*, immediately comes to mind. The protagonist is a sort of roguish Argentinian character who leads a vagabond existence. In this story, Payró has the various dialects interfere in the dialogues of the Italian immigrants, thereby creating a hybridized narrative while reshaping his native Spanish to open it up to the contaminations put forward by the immigrants themselves. For example, there is a particular dialogue that I like to recall, in which the character Laucha goes to see a Neapolitan priest in an attempt to arrange a false marriage with an Italian widow. (The following is the published English translation from the original Spanish):

> "Whatcha wanna?" he asked me.
> "Fine! Fine! S'ten nationalli . . . And who you marry?
>         . . . Gotta pay down for the banns . . .
> . Girl around here? . . . Eh! . . . S'what I said . . . ten nationalli and cheap at the price!"
> "Wait a minute, Father! . . . I wanted the . . . how do you call it?—Oh, yes, the banns waived . . ."
> "S'thirty!"
> "And to marry us at the bride's house . . ."
> "Sixty! . . . No cheaper."
> "Oh, that doesn't matter, Father: you'll get the sixty pesos . . . But, when could you marry us?"
> "Any time you wanna . . . She promish?"
> "She what?"
> "The girl . . ."

"Ah! Yes! Doña Carolina, the widow, do you know?
    Of the Polvadera ..."
"Fine, fine ..."[2]

Payró's realism, and the general comic style, requires him to take a stand regarding the language in such a way that all the social classes are clearly represented through their modes of expression. Payró seeks to enliven his language with the help of other languages. In fact, it is precisely this hybridization that gives rise to the social implications of the story.

Along similar lines, there is another Argentinian writer, Roberto Raschella (the Spanish translator of Italian classics) who writes in a quasi-hybrid language interspersed with spoken Italian. I am referring in particular to two books of his: *Diálogos en los patios rojos* (Dialogues in the red courtyard) (1994) and *Si hubiéramos vivido aquí* (If we had lived here) (1998). In these two works, the challenge for Raschella is not to give voice to the various spoken idioms in Argentina, but rather to create a foreign language within his own Spanish as if he were an Italian writer who has lost his mother tongue and is trying to express himself in Spanish all the while dragging behind him his semantic and linguistic baggage. Therefore, not a recreation of a spoken language with foreign interference, but a much wider challenge that takes language to its very limits until it transforms it from within. In other words, you could say that Raschella confers on Spanish an entirely Italian musicality and timbre.

Paradoxically, when writing in a language similar to our mother tongue the first hurdle we face is presented by that very similarity because we always tend to take with us our own syntactical heritage and then apply it to the new language. At times, knowing how to manipulate this kind of *foreignness* can have some interesting results, for example as in Roberto Raschella's *Dialogos en los patios rojos* cited above. However, at other times the results can be disastrous.

It would be easier, I imagine, even though I have no direct experience in the matter, to change register entirely. (I'm thinking of the passage from one language to a dissimilar one such as that of Italian into English or German). However, whether similar or not, a foreigner is always hunting for a language. The quarry is that ferocious beast, often out of reach that lies hidden behind all idioms. Every foreigner has to measure himself against this risk, this hunt. The language we speak and write is a map that has to be slowly created and that, in the final analysis, we never finish drawing. A map that essentially plots out our hunt for "that fleeing beast" that is language.

# ∽ 20 ∽

# Every Foreigner Is in Their Own Way a Translator

On the eve of the five hundredth anniversary of the discovery of America a professor from the Caribbean was invited by an historical society from Macerata to speak on the role of Doña Marina commonly known as La Malinche, who was both Hernan Cortez's interpreter and lover during the conquest of Mexico. One of the lecture organizers happened to be a friend who was studying philosophy with me, and she invited me to participate. I thought it might be interesting and so I accepted saying I would happily go along. Also because, as I explained to my friend, La Malinche was considered the first *translator* but also the first *traitor* in the history of Latin America.

The next day I ran into this friend again and she asked me, seeing that this Caribbean professor did not speak any Italian, if I could translate "a few words" she said: "But only if we in the audience don't fully understand the Spanish." I agreed, even though I knew beforehand that I would be consumed by shyness. (Let me add that, alas, I am incapable of refusing an invitation or an offer even when I would prefer not to accept.)

Well, that afternoon—I still remember it, I think I shall remember it until my dying day—a lot of people showed up for the lecture. When I arrived, after the initial greetings and presentations, I was introduced as *the translator*, and I was asked to sit next to the Caribbean speaker. After a series of thanks on the part of the authorities, the professor who was tall and had very intense, dark eyes, began his lecture on Doña Marina known as La Malinche.

He began with a short introduction to the Mexican princess and then, at a certain point, when he thought he had said enough, he turned to me on his left. I then turned to him (he was on my right), perhaps I even gave him a little smile, I can't remember. Then I looked at the audience in front of me, who in turn were looking at me, expecting me to translate into Italian the entire introduction to the Mexican princess. In that very moment I wanted nothing more than for the floor to swallow me up, or I would have thanked all the angels in heaven if they had pierced me with a lightning bolt. There followed some polite coughing, nervous giggles, perplexed looks, the usual things people do when they see that someone is in difficulty. Never had I felt such a foreigner, such a stranger in my life.

Julia Kristeva in a chapter of her book, *The Future of a Revolt*, believes that changing language means losing one's *nature*, betraying or translating it. "The foreigner," she writes, "is essentially a translator."[1] In that moment, though, I only felt like a failed translator, speechless, stricken silent, as if I no longer knew any language at all. And yet, during the two years I had been in Italy, I considered my new language a pretext for rebirth, because I was rooting my identity in the language that was at this moment rejecting me and in which I could not even stammer a few words. I had no idea how to deal with those stares, those expectations regarding my role.

Maybe this was the price that I had to pay for that crime of matricide I had committed when I decided to leave my country of origin? Perhaps I was now La Malinche, translator or traitor who did not know the language well enough? How would I be able to transform myself into that ideal translator who doesn't reveal the slightest trace of their mother tongue? In the end, I spoke up and asked if it was necessary for me to translate what the Caribbean speaker had said, expecting them to say no, that they had completely understood the lecture. Instead, they all said yes, it was necessary to translate it because it was not at all clear to anybody. And so, in this traumatic fashion, my conflicted relationship with Italian was born and possibly also my terror of using a foreign language in public.

## ~ 21 ~

# Some Cases of
# Self-Translation

In 1955 Juan Rodolfo Wilcock left Argentina definitively and settled in Rome. In that same period, another Argentine, Hector Bianciotti, left his homeland to go and settle in Paris and subsequently to write in French. A few years after his arrival in Italy, Wilcock published *Chaos* (1960), a collection of short stories from the mid-forties to the mid-fifties originally written in Spanish—his first book in Italian, which he himself translated from Spanish. In 1963 he published—this time in Italian—a collection of poems entitled *Poesie spagnole* (Spanish poems), an anthology that Wilcock created from his six books of poetry previously published in Argentina between 1940 and 1951. This was not a case of rewriting, such as Beckett's self-translations into his mother tongue, that is, from French into English, or of Witold Gombrow-icz's *Ferdydurke* from Polish into Spanish.

Wilcock's self-translation is poetically faithful to the original even in those instances where he, as the author, might have allowed himself to subvert the code of ethics that forces every translator to respect the original (the poems are published with the two texts side by side to indicate a kind of mimesis in the transposition from Spanish into Italian). Wilcock is aware that to write in a language other than our mother tongue presupposes a revisitation of the places, the syntax and rhythms in light of the new language. He does so with mastery without succumbing to Spanish-influenced solutions. In the introduction to the *Poesie spagnole* he refers to himself in the third person: "In the face of a language that is corrupted and perverted by platitudes, no less than by the inextricable sleaze ironically called *fine writing*, the young writer feels first and foremost the need to create a new language for himself."[1]

It is precisely in this *new language* that has welcomed him that Wilcock will write all his books from the sixties on: his imaginary chronicles, his translations of Marlowe's plays and of the beginning of *Finnegans Wake* published in 1961 in the complete works of Joyce edited by Giacomo Debenedetti. (Unlike Wilcock, Héctor Bianciotti never translated his own novels written in Spanish into French before he switched languages. There is, in this choice of his, a kind of impossibility to self-translate.) Moreover, Wilcock's self-translations can be seen as bearing witness to the linguistic mutation that preceded his definitive move to Italian. Once he crossed that frontier, he abandoned Spanish, and he no longer felt the need, as Beckett did, to self-translate into his mother tongue. As Wilcock stated at the end of his introduction to the translated volume (always in the third person): "With his choice of career now confirmed and his reputation completely ruined, the writer turned to easy living, to reading, to the distractions of exile and of the theater. Then, in 1958, driven by an unusual series of events, he decided to switch both his language and his public, and so by resorting to linguistic balancing acts he began to write in a kind of Italian."[2]

One year after the publication of *Poesie spagnole* Wilcock met Pier Paolo Pasolini, who cast him in the role of Caiaphas in his film *The Gospel According to Matthew*. Let me stop for a moment and stay with Pasolini to continue the subject of self-translation, but in a different register from that of Wilcock.

In 1942, while studying humanities at the University of Bologna, Pasolini self-published a collection of poems titled *Poesia a Casarsa* (Poetry in Casarsa) through the *Libreria Antiquaria Mario Landi* in Bologna. In 1954, these poems were included in Pasolini's *La meglio gioventù (The Best of Youth)* that he dedicated to literary critic Gianfranco Contini. It is a slim volume, the first work that Pasolini published, written in the dialect of Friuli, a northeastern region of Italy, and spoken in Casarsa, transmitted orally, without a written form. Even though it was not his mother tongue, the Friulian dialect of Casarsa, spoken mainly in the countryside, gave Pasolini the chance to come face to face with a pure language, which he transcribed for the first time. *Poetry in Casarsa*, just like the entire collection of *The Best of Youth*, is an important text because Pasolini builds his own *linguistic maternity* around this adopted language. In the appendix to the 1942 edition, Pasolini wrote: "The Friulian *idio* [idiom] of these poems, is not the genuine one, but the one gently intermingled with the language of the Veneto which is spoken on the right bank of the Tagliamento; furthermore, the force I have applied to it, to constrain it within poetic meter and diction, is not slight."[3]

With this text Pasolini inaugurates Italian neo-dialectic poetry. In 1975, a few months before Pasolini's death, *The Best of Youth* was published (his last book while he was alive) that reproduced the early edition of the Friulian poetry, with some additions and revisions, all accompanied by his self-translation.

To summarize, Pasolini twice revisits this collection of poems in two fundamental moments of his career as a writer: the first when he initially published it, the other, the edition that came out just before his death. I find it interesting that in such a turbulent life and writing career, the beginning and the end can be traced in some way to his poetic search for a *linguistic maternity* and to the problem of self-translation of this Friulian idiom into Italian, of this eternally sought-after mother tongue recreated on the written page. However, Pasolini does not translate the Friulian poems into Italian verse. Perhaps his choice to include a prose translation at the bottom of the page has to do with the impossibility of translating poetry or with the impossibility of self-translation, of turning into Italian a language that the writer himself defines as "an absolute language, inexistent in nature" (I quote from the note to *The Best of Youth*, 124) And yet, these last prose self-translations are interwoven with verse: the rhyme is not sacrificed, the translations capture well that Friulian voice of the original text, that tension between the rhythm of the spoken idiom and the dialect articulation. In some way they complete the original and never lessen it.

In 1939, a shipping company invited the Polish writer Witold Gombrowicz to travel on the inaugural voyage between Gydynia/Gdansk and Buenos Aires. During what was supposed to be a short sojourn in Buenos Aires, the Second World War broke out, and he stayed on until 1963: "Alone, lost, cut off, alien, unknown, a drowned man. My eardrums were still being assailed by the feverish din of European radio speakers, I was still being assaulted by the wartime roar of newspapers, and already I was immersing myself in an incomprehensible speech and in a life quite remote from my former one. Which is what is called an uncommon moment."[4]

Thus he writes in one of his diaries, considered by many to be one of his fundamental works. During those twenty-four years, although he continued to write in Polish, Gombrowicz became a major Argentinian writer. In fact, Ricardo Piglia proclaimed that *Trans-Atlantyk* was one of the best novels written in Argentina, the first novel that the Polish writer wrote in exile, in his mother tongue, which by then he was using exclusively in his writings like a kind of idiolect. What would have happened, asked Piglia, if Gombrowicz had written *Trans-Atlantyk* in Spanish? Would he have become the Argentinian Conrad? In the translation of *Ferdydurke* published in 1947 in Buenos Aires, there remained an important trace of the relationship that Gombrowicz established with both languages, Polish and Spanish. The first edition had come out in Warsaw in 1938 and had been well received in Polish literary circles thanks to its stylistic originality.

In the first draft of the Argentinian *Ferdydurke*, though, Gombrowicz experiments with a new form, a kind of slavicized Spanish, stretching it to the limits of the language with the intention of forcing the words and the syntax to eventually accept other meanings and semantic shifts. So, for Gombrowicz it was not a search for hypothetical equivalents of the original text, considered the definitive one, but rather an ultimate elaboration, a revisitation in the light of the new language, a *Ferdydurke* parallel to the Polish one: a different book, a new version based on the original edition.

Gombrowicz wanted to imbue his text with a different breath, drawn from this new experience of exile ("This translation is my own and bears only a distant resemblance to the original text," he wrote in the preface to the 1947 edition) without considering the original as a point of arrival; on the contrary, the original became the basis for his conquest of the Spanish language. This specific feature differentiates him from Wilcock's own technique and approach who, as we saw, wrote in his mother tongue and self-translated into Italian remaining faithful to the original text.

Behind this translation there is another story: in the Chess Room at the Café Rex in Buenos Aires on the Avenida Corrientes, each day a translation committee used to meet, including the Cuban writer, Virgilio Piñera. This committee would discuss the various versions of the translation, recounts Gombrowicz in his preface. None of Gombrowicz's friends knew Polish; however, when Spanish could no longer accept contortions, they resorted to French. The echo of this story is taken up and relaunched by Piglia in *Crítica y ficción* (Criticism and fiction): "The Argentinian novel is therefore a Polish one: I mean, a Polish novel translated into a future Spanish in a café in Buenos Aires by a band of conspirators led by an apocryphal count."[5]

I do not think it inappropriate to juxtapose Gombrowicz's *Ferdydurke* with Joyce's translation into Italian of two excerpts from *Finnegans Wake* that are part of the chapter known as "Anna Livia Plurabelle." *Finnegans Wake* came out in English in 1939, and Joyce translated these passages in 1938–1939 in collaboration with Nino Frank, a young antifascist who had a role that was similar to Virgilio Piñera's for Gombrowicz. As Jacqueline Risset wrote in her introduction to *James Joyce, Scritti italiani* (James Joyce, Italian writings) in Joyce's self-translation of these excerpts two levels of writing intersect: "the double experience of dialect, especially of the Triestino dialect that he spoke in his own family, and of the earliest, highest level of literary Italian (the Italian of Dante) enables Joyce to understand the essentially plural aspect of this language, with great assurance."[6] Joyce's intention was to give as much orality as possible to the washerwomen's vernacular gossip, in other words, a speech tied to rhythm and to invention, rather than to fidelity to the text. The English version of *Finnegans Wake,* written in a kind of invented language and impossible to translate, becomes the starting point for a revisitation that further emphasizes the spoken register.

Beckett takes up again the English language that he had abandoned after the death of his mother. He takes it up again only in order to translate what he had written in French. However, "what he does," writes Nadia Fusini in her introduction to the Italian translation of Beckett's *Mal vu mal dit*, "might not be called a real translation. Rather, it is the birth of a new text, the second incarnation of something that, even though of the same flesh, now claims another."[7]

Thus, English becomes a rediscovered language, to which Beckett returned to compare it with the works written in his adopted language. He creates in French and reinterprets it in the light of the language of his infancy. In this way he loses his mother tongue—which is not a creative language, but an interpretive one for him—only to find it again years later. This is the fruit of a revisitation, of a rewriting (often not consented to a translator who does not have to confront himself with his own work). But Beckett does not self-translate; he recreates the text. His self-translation is not a repetition of the original work, it is a different interpretation. His intent is that neither of the two languages cast its shadow on the other, both when he self-translates from English into French and vice versa. "So, are they two works? Or doubles? Is one the original? The other a translation? Or are they two versions, the first being a rough draft, the second the final version?" Nadia Fusini asks herself. His translation is not secondary to the original one. He does not self-translate like Wilcock. This is not a reincarnation or a continuation revisited by another language. He uses his mother tongue like an instrument of free translation: "From that foreign language he tries to redeem that language that is buried within it, a prisoner, and the imprisoned language is liberated in the translation. In liberating itself we discover that it speaks English rather than French," concludes Nadia Fusini. Derek Walcott, commenting on Brodsky's self-translations of his poems, says something similar:

> One feels that Brodsky wishes the book to be read as English verse, not as translated Russian. . . . For a poet to translate himself involves not only a change of language but what translation literally means, a crossing to another place, an accommodation of temperament, a shadowing of sensibility as the original poem poses at the frontier. . . . What is extraordinary, in fact phenomenal in its effort, is the determination to render, almost to deliver, the poem from its original language into the poetry of the new country. To give the one work, simultaneously, two mother tongues.[8]

Beckett, too, seems to be dealing with two mother tongues. His self-translations tend therefore to improve on the creative act, as is the case with *Mal vu mal dit* transformed into

*Ill Seen, Ill Said.* In this second birth of the text, a kind of triumph takes place, in the sense that Beckett's English is an infinitely richer, more malleable and fresh language and, as Nadia Fusini points out: "The language, rediscovered after being refuted, dances with wondrous ease and vivacity. Yes, Beckett's English is more beautiful than his French."[9]

# ～ 22 ～

# Identity and National Language

The age-old problem of cultural identity has long plagued Latin American countries and their writers. In fact, until the 1980s, no Latin American author ever drew back from confronting the issue of personal identity. Already in the early 1800s, in Argentina it was landscape that defined identity, an identity that sprang from a close connection to the land. The ultimate landscape was the desert, and the desert evoked dreams and illusions. "The desert, limitless, wide open and mysterious spread out at his feet," are the first lines of the epic poem *La cautiva* (The captive woman) by Esteban Echeverría, the poet who introduced Romanticism to Argentina.

The desert has a precise meaning, it has a physical, natural dimension, but the desert here is also the space occupied by people whose culture was never recognized. It is closely connected to an ideology that culminated in 1879 with the famous Conquest of the Desert, an Argentinian military campaign led by General Roca. On the one hand it implied the suppression of the Indigenous peoples (the Mapuches, the Tehuelches, the Ranqueles, among others). On the other hand, it signaled the definitive annexation of the Pampas and of Patagonia into the Argentine nation, without, however, recognizing the rights of the peoples who had always lived on those lands and for whom, obviously, it was not a desert. And yet Argentina was founded on the concept of the *Other*, but an *Other* who was predetermined, politically chosen: the working immigrant, not the native inhabitant. Immigration was a necessary condition for the building of the nation and of its identity, starting from Argentinian independence all the way to the mid-1800s.

This relationship with the *Other* was not considered a threat, but rather a promise. The two almost opposing worlds that had existed until then, the one Hispanic-creole, the other indigenous, were not enough to build a nation: a European influx was needed. Furthermore, Argentina did not stem from a single, ancient root, unlike Mexico or Peru (products of the meeting or the opposition of two strong roots that had destabilized native identity). Argentina's root was, to quote Glissant, *rhizomatic*, that is, a root that does not grow deep underground but spreads out growing around other roots.

Therefore, Argentinian cultural identity was the result, on the one hand, of the negation of a pre-existing culture (that of the indigenous people); on the other hand, it was the result of the break from Spain. Lastly, it was the result of a meeting with various European cultures. Thus, it was in this context that, after gaining political independence from

Spain, Argentina sought linguistic independence through the recovery of orality.

There are numerous cases of language creolization founded on orality. An example is the work of Ahmadou Kourouma, the writer from the Ivory Coast, who used a different rhythm, register, and lexicon to create a new Ivorian version of French through Malinke, his mother tongue. Similarly, in Argentina, immediately following independence, the Spanish language had become an obstacle to be overcome. In 1837, in his inaugural speech at the Literary Salon in Buenos Aires, Juan Maria Gutiérrez stated: "We must divorce ourselves from the Spaniards. We must emancipate ourselves from peninsular traditions, as we were able to do in the matter of politics when we proclaimed ourselves free. We remain tied still through the strong and tight bond of language; but it will loosen day by day. . . . And if we are to have a literature, let us make it a national one; so that it may represent our customs and our nature. . . . Just as our lakes and fast-moving rivers reflect in their waters only the stars of our hemisphere."[1]

Those stars were also the many languages of the immigrants. But not only: they also represented their view of the world. Thus, a linguistic conscience was born that took diversity into account. As Juan Bautista Alberdi, the guiding spirit of the Argentine constitution wrote: "Our language yearns for emancipation because it is one of the many faces of our national emancipation."[2]

In one way or another, all communities have been constituted in their own language. In this situation, the poet par excellence would be the one to affirm the uniqueness of the community, a uniqueness that is always elusive and hard to grasp, but that knows how to accept contaminations and nuances. Therefore, a country's identity is linguistic before it is political. Argentina had to be invented, nothing from its pre-Hispanic or colonial past could be recycled in this process of modernization. There was a whole desert waiting to be filled up: "So, at the origin of Argentinian culture there is the desert," writes Beatriz Sarlo, "This is not a descriptive proposition, it is an ideological one: it is the way in which intellectuals lived their relationship with society, with the *Other* and with those who were different."[3] Therefore, the construction of a past, even a linguistic past, becomes necessary. But we do not know if it was the desert that founded Argentinian literature or vice versa.

Consequently, immigration opens up this cycle of historical reconstruction creating a dichotomy between an *inside* (a world populated by indigenous people) and an *outside* (European immigrants). What we want to negate and what we want to welcome. There is an old saying that is quoted every time people talk about Argentinian identity: "Mexicans are descended from the Aztecs; Peruvians are descended from the Incas, and Argentinians are descended from ships." Those ships that, for a century, arrived in the Port of Buenos Aires bursting with immigrants and hapless dreamers. The indigenous or pre-Hispanic world is hardly ever mentioned. The gaze is always focused on the port and never towards those inner borders that kept the indigenous peoples away from civilization.

In Italy instead, it was not a nation that produced a literature, but the opposite. Literature and language were the harbingers of the future Italian nation. Italy, we might say, was among the first to have a language and the last to have a nation. I have always been intrigued by the fact that Italian has remained close to its linguistic origins throughout the centuries. It has always amazed me that an Italian (and now me too) can read St. Francis's *Canticle of the Creatures* (written in 1224, one of the earliest Italian texts) without needing a translation because the inner structure of Italian has remained almost identical. This is not the case for a Spaniard who wants to read *El Cid*, also written in that same period, or someone French wanting to read *The Song of Roland*. The story of Italy, one could say, is the story of a language and a literature that took hold, not through political power, but through culture, with its manuscripts and its books. Italian literary critic Gian Luigi Beccaria explained that the texts of the three major authors of the 1300s, Dante, Petrarch, and Boccaccio, formed the basis of the unified literary canon for Italian writers.

Yet Italian was not a native tongue: the mother tongue was that *grammar of feelings*, the dialects. The fact that starting in the 1300s Italian was established as a relatively shared literary language in the whole peninsula, while being unable to rely on a unifying spoken language, should make us all proud both to write and speak Italian today. Perhaps for me, it was a necessity: I had to abandon my mother tongue in order to discover this tangle of dialects, of written languages, of spoken languages, all called *Italian* to try to find my way in this labyrinth of hidden panthers and lost scents.

## ~ 23 ~

# The Language of Death

On October 28, 1964, in an interview with Günther Gaus that was part of the series *Zur Person* (About the person) on German TV Channel 2, Hannah Arendt answered a series of questions mainly concerning her abandonment of Germany in 1933. When at one point, Günther Gaus asked her what she still retained from pre-Hitlerian Germany, Arendt declared, with no hesitation: her strong, unconditional attachment to the German language:

GAUS: And that means a great deal to you.

ARENDT: A great deal. I have always consciously refused to lose my mother tongue. I have always maintained a certain distance from French, which I then spoke very well, as well as from English, which I write today.

GAUS: I wanted to ask you that. You write in English now?

ARENDT: I write in English, but I have never lost a feeling of distance from it. There is a tremendous difference between your mother tongue and another language. For myself I can put it extremely simply: In German I know a large part of German poetry by heart.[1]

For many exiles, though, after Auschwitz German became a hostile language to be forgotten. This was the case for Hans Schwarz, for instance, the character in Fred Uhlman's *Reunited* who emigrated from Stuttgart to the United States where he created a new life for himself and tried to forget his past, including his mother tongue: "Of course I can still speak the language perfectly well . . . but I dislike it. My wounds have not healed and to be reminded of Germany is to have salt rubbed into them."[2] This character's tragedy is inextricably interwoven with his author's life. In fact, Uhlman had abandoned Swabia in 1933 to move first to Paris and then, three years later, to the UK. His autobiography, titled *The Making of an Englishman*, underscores his change of language and nationality.

We also notice this hostility towards German in *The Diary of Anne Frank*. In her entry of Tuesday, November 17, 1942, Anne tells of the arrival of dentist Albert Dussel to the Dutch hiding place at the Van Daan's home where German exiles sought refuge. On the day of his arrival he is given a typed set of rules titled "Prospectus and Guide to the Secret Annex." One of the entries regards languages: *Use of language*: it is necessary to speak softly at all times. Only the language of civilized people may be spoken, thus no German.[3]

In contrast, Hannah Arendt cannot detach herself from German, quite the opposite: she refuses to lose it. She considers German the place she belongs to, her *Heimat*, her homeland. She will never lose German because, as she stated in the aforementioned interview: "It wasn't the German language that went crazy. And, second, there is no substitution for the mother tongue."[4]

After mentioning the impossibility of substituting one's mother tongue, Hannah Arendt adds: "People can forget their mother tongue. That's true—I have seen it. There are people who speak the new language better than I do. I still speak with a very heavy accent, and I often speak unidiomatically. They can all do these things correctly. But they do them in a language in which one cliché chases another because the productivity that one has in one's own language is cut off when one forgets that language" (ibid).

When the interviewer asked her whether this forgetting could be "the result of a repression," Hannah Arendt replied that the substitution of one's language is the consequence of a repression due, perhaps, to a sort of defense against one's own language: "I have seen it in people as a result of shock. You know, what was decisive was not the year 1933, at least not for me. What was decisive was the day we learned about Auschwitz." Auschwitz, or more precisely, the moment people become aware of the existence of such a place, becomes the site of the fracture, of an absolute loss, of what "ought not to have happened." Yet, Hannah Arendt emphasizes that "The German language is the essential thing that has remained and that I have always consciously preserved."

German is the language that makes her feel rooted in her birthplace; language is the soil in which distance is nurtured, the only remaining essential element. In his 1958 acceptance speech for the Bremen Literary Prize, Paul Celan wrote: "Only one thing remained reachable, close and secure amid all losses: language."[5] That language, German, in which Celan decided to write, was the language of his mother who had been deported and died along with her husband after being picked up in one of the Sabbath night raids in Cernăuți, Romania (now Chernivtsi, Ukraine). German, at the same time, was the language of the persecutors who had deported his mother. He could have chosen to write in Romanian or French (he had gone into exile in Paris in 1948), but he preferred to write in German, a language that was close to him yet, at the same time, foreign, fractured. It was a language that could exterminate yet save, that rose above the horizon of his daily life experienced in French. German, therefore, was the language of the mother transformed into the language of death.

Talking about Celan and the unicity of language for a poet in the chapter "The Idea of the Unique," included in his volume *Idea of Prose*, Giorgio Agamben writes: "And when in Bucharest just after the war his friends tried to convince him to become a Romanian poet (his Romanian poems of that period have survived), on the grounds that he should not write in the language of the murderers of his parents who died in a Nazi concentration camp, Celan simply replied: "It is only in one's mother tongue that one can tell the truth. In a foreign language the poet lies."[6]

Celan's reply to his Romanian friends emphasizes that belief: truth dwells in that mother tongue that he never lost and still uses. As he explains: "In this language I tried, during those years and the years after, to write poems: in order to speak, to orient myself, to find out where I was, where I was going, to chart my reality. It meant movement, you see, something happening, being *en route*, an attempt to find a direction" (*Collected Prose*, 34). Celan creates his own language within German in order to transcend it and to question the sense of the story fate reserved for him or, as Celan himself said, to bring it to light: "Through the thousand darknesses of murderous speech" (34).

German philosopher Theodor Adorno also wanted "to go on loving the German language, to go on cultivating that originary intimacy with his idiom-but without nationalism, without the collective narcissism (kollektiven Narzissmus) of a *metaphysics* of language."[7]

On the other hand, Jean Améry (pseudonym of Hans Chaim Mayer) who survived Auschwitz and wrote an analysis on defeat and the spirit of his time based on his experience, goes as far as feeling he no longer belongs to his *Heimat*. In *At the Mind's Limit. Contemplations by a Survivor on Auschwitz and Its Realities,* one of the most cogent texts on the subject, he wrote: "We were shut out from German reality and therefore also from the German language."[8] In 1945, Améry moved to Brussels and for the rest of his life maintained a close relationship with his mother tongue: "Daily, in spite of extreme aversion, I read the *Brüsseler Zeitung,* the organ of the German occupying power in the West" (53). Yet, he immediately realized he had lost his sense of belonging, or perhaps never had it to begin with, because everything that had to do with Germany was a major misunderstanding: "The words were laden with a given reality, which was the threat of death" (53).

His mother tongue, at a certain point, becomes hostile, perfidious, obscured by an irreparable loss, and the foreign language does not provide the necessary welcome to make up for this loss. In that book, Améry tries to reconstruct and understand what the loss of the *Heimat* means for an exile from the Third Reich. *Heimat* intended as homeland, mother tongue and narrative space. Only in 1935, did he realize he was a Jew, only after the promulgation of the Nuremberg Race Laws asserting the superiority of the Aryan race and legalizing the persecution of Jews. From that moment on he realizes he is a man who can no longer say *we*: a man with no land, no rights and struck by a curse: "Home is the land of one's childhood and youth. Whoever has lost it remains lost himself. Even if he has learned not to stumble about in the foreign country as if he were drunk, but rather to tread the ground with some fearlessness" (48). Foreigners live an incomplete condition. They are never fully in one place and constantly experience an inner displacement. Jean Améry feels this sense of disorientation: "If one has no home, however, one becomes subject to disorder, confusion, desultoriness." (47). In a poem published in 1884, "Abschied" ("Farewell"), Nietzsche also evokes this sense of loss:

> The crows caw
> And move in whirring flight to the city:
> Soon it will snow,
> Woe betide [*Weh dem*] he who has no home![9]

Améry shows us that it was not the oppressors but rather the victims of Auschwitz who remained locked in that sphere of homeland that no longer existed. While Hannah Arendt succeeded in regaining her mother tongue, because in her opinion "It wasn't the German language that went crazy," Améry cannot decontextualize it from his more recent story, the one fate reserved for him.

In *At the Mind's Limit* he recalls an anecdote from 1943, a short time before his arrest in Belgium. He was printing leaflets in an apartment with some other exiles. One day an SS officer who lived in the apartment below, bothered by the noise above, climbed the stairs, knocked on the door, and shouted at them to be quiet. He used the dialect spoken in Améry's region, heard in that moment by Améry for the first time in many years. He was tempted to answer in the same dialect, but in the end, answered in French so as not to reveal his identity: "At that moment I understood *completely* and forever that my home was enemy country and that the good comrade was sent here from the hostile homeland to wipe me out."[10]

# ~ 24 ~

# Language as Property

The anecdote recounted by Jean Améry may well explain how our own language, during exile, can become a threat. Suddenly the *Heimat* is transformed into a place of non-belonging. So, we have to reject our mother tongue, hide it—remember the Ephramites—because our own language is transformed into the language of the *Other* and from our mother tongue it has become the death language, or rather, the language of death. However, can we consider language a natural possession of this or that group? To whom does it belong? Can we barricade it inside a community of speakers?

The immediate reaction is to say that a language belongs to no one; it belongs to whoever speaks it, and that those who speak it do not possess it; rather we belong to the language, we share it without claiming dominion over it. It is language that possesses us. We are inside language the way the swallow is in the air, because, like the air, language is the locus of opening, an opening that on one hand, allows no possession, and on the other, no autonomy.

"My language, the only one I hear myself speak and agree to speak, is the language of the Other,"[1] wrote Jacques Derrida in his autobiography *Monolingualism of the Other OR The Prosthesis of Origin*. This book is entirely constructed around the problem of being able to be monolingual and yet speak a language that is not your own. As a French Jew born in Algeria, when he was a child Derrida only knew the *official language* because his community had lost all ties with the Jewish tradition and with the local languages. And yet, between 1940 and 1943, the Jewish community in Algeria lost their French citizenship, which, in turn had been imposed on them, without the possibility of acquiring another: "I am speaking of a "community" group (a "mass" assembling together tens or hundreds of thousands of persons), a supposedly "ethnic" or religious" group that one day finds itself deprived, as a group, of its citizenship by a state that, with the brutality of a unilateral decision withdraws it without asking for their opinion, and without the said group gaining back any other citizenship. No other" (15).

Taking his cue from this condition of being an *expatriate*—in the very land of his birth—Derrida meditates on the concept of citizenship and on the nature of power, based not on politics but on the question of the mother tongue. A language that is never his and that never will be: "I have but one language—yet that language is not mine," he wrote at the beginning of the text. Not only because it is the language of the *Other* (a language that belongs exclusively to the French) but above all because it is language that possesses us: "I am monolingual. My monolingualism dwells, and I call it my dwelling; it feels like one to me, and I remain in it and inhabit it. It inhabits me. The monolingualism in which I draw my very breath is, for me, my element. Not a natural element, not the transparency of the ether, but an absolute habitat. It is impassable, indisputable: I cannot challenge it except by testifying to its omnipresence in me. It would always have preceded me. It is me. For me, this monolingualism is me" (1).

We have no right of possession on language. Declaring it *ours* only means that we belong to it because I am not the one who speaks it, but rather, it is that particular language that bestows on me the identifying name of *I*. In this way our mother tongue becomes the most intimate, but at the same time, the most foreign to us, precisely because it is *Other*.

# ~ 25 ~

# The Abandonment
of Language

In his book, *On the Death and Life of Languages*, Claude Hagège, makes the following observation: "Among the Angmassalik, an Eskimo population in Southwest Greenland, some who are old and dying change their last name in an attempt to avoid death's reach. Unable to identify them by their usual names, death will not know where to find them."[1] So by rebaptizing themselves (we're not talking about a real baptism, but about a new naming) they can escape fate, precisely because there is a belief that the identity of each and every individual is concealed beneath their name. Therefore, by changing their name they can become someone other than who they were. On the one hand, they lose their identity, because the original name no longer corresponds to any soul or body; on the other, however, they acquire a new existence that might give them back the freedom that they did not have under the other name.

A similar case to that of the Angmassalik, but with a different social connotation, can be found among certain Japanese, who by reason of financial difficulties (debts, extortions, layoffs, and so on) decide to disappear in order to create a new life elsewhere and to cut themselves off from their past: the *Johatsu*, which in Japanese means "Evaporated People," people who disappear into nothing. It would seem that in Japan it is possible to "become another," changing from what one was before encountering financial difficulties.

So, what remains of all this once we have changed our identity (either because we are being hounded by death or by our creditors)? We can do without our physical traits (there are those who do so without being hounded at all). We can also do without our usual behavior or habits, but we can never change our own linguistic identity, because it is part of our very being. We inhabit our language, it contains us in its shell, whatever our name might be. It is not purely a means of communication; language reveals us in our essence and in our very intimate being. Apart from substituting one's name or nationality, there may be a variety of reasons why people change language, at times even abandoning it. Claude Hagège analyzes a few cases. For example, the case of the Tlingit community in southeast Alaska in which parents refuse to teach their own language to their children for fear that it might stigmatize them: "To still speak Tlingit is to risk appearing like a half-wit or a peasant, and they fear that teaching this language to children will hinder not only their learning English at an early age, but also their mental development" (136). Moreover, they believe that by teaching Tlingit to their children they would keep alive certain traditional beliefs that they would prefer to leave behind. The same thing happens with the Rama in Nicaragua, who go so far as to consider their language not even a language, which they are ashamed to speak.

There are many people who are convinced that their own language is unable to give voice to modern life and they prefer to abandon it, thus allowing their particular beliefs and traditions to die, and then submit to another language that will never be able to express their particular culture. Not only are there examples of voluntary abandonment but even cases of authentic "linguicides" where the powers that be, without necessarily exterminating the speakers, block the spreading of that language. In the words of Hegège: "State linguicide . . . is illustrated by the war the United States waged during the first decades of the twentieth century on the languages spoken on the various islands of Micronesia, like Chamorro (or Guameño) on Guam, as well as other languages on Saipan, Rota, Tinian, Pagan, Anatahan, and Alamagan" (119).

The examples proliferate in the twentieth century during the colonial period in which many languages were targeted and attacked as being demonic. In Alaska, as in the example above, at the beginning of the 1900s the use of native languages as a means of instruction was banned. Various cases of linguicide have been documented in the course of history forcing indigenous peoples to change language. In 1616, says Hagège, the Scottish Parliament passed a law in favor of English with the aim of substituting it for Scottish Gaelic, "declared the source of all barbarity" (120). Consequently, the Scottish Gaelic language was to be suppressed and banished from every type of instruction.

At times, a language is abandoned simply as a matter of survival, as was the case of Pipil in El Salvador in 1932 at the time of the *gran matanza*, the great massacre, when 25,000 native inhabitants were slaughtered (and with them disappeared the Cacaopera and the Lenca languages). The Pipil speakers, seeing that they were about to suffer the same fate of the Cacaopera and Lenca speakers, decided to renounce their tongue, and today Pipil is in all likelihood, extinct.

Every year twenty-five languages die. Globalization means not only the transformation of commerce but also of the lives of entire populations. The extinction of any language, no matter which, even of the most rare or unknown, even the language spoken by Landolfi's character Y, the sole speaker (see Chapter 13) constitutes an impoverishment, a fundamental loss for us all.

The death of a language also kills everything that cannot exist without being named by a language. Therefore, such a disappearance also presupposes the extinction of a world, of a point of view and a perspective, even when dealing with a mixed or creole language. Not only does a language disappear, but also the processes of contamination and of relationships among its peoples disappear. Languages are born (we don't understand exactly when, but at some point, they are), and maybe one day, following the destiny of peoples, they will perish and others will take their place, with other perspectives and other limits. Not one language can be considered eternal. Franz Rosenzweig has something to add on the subject: "The language of the peoples follows with utmost subtlety the vital changes of destinies of the people, but this following of the living also pulls language into the destiny of the living, to die."[2]

## ~ 26 ~

# The Difficulty of Abandoning One's Own Language

In his autobiographical memoir, *Speak, Memory*, Nabokov writes that during his Cambridge, UK exile (after leaving first St. Petersburg in 1917 and then Crimea in 1919) he dedicated himself entirely to literature, foregoing all other things, including politics. In his "Cambridge rooms" he read the "Song of Igor's Campaign," . . . the poetry of Pushkin and Tyutchev, the prose of Gogol and Tolstoy, . . . the Russian naturalists who had explored and described the wilds of central Asia."[1]

One day, at a bookstall in the Market Place he found a second-hand copy of Dahl's *Interpretative Dictionary of the Living Russian Language* in four volumes. He bought it in the hope of reading at least ten pages a day: "My fear of losing or corrupting, through alien influence, the only thing I had salvaged from Russia—her language—became positively morbid and considerably more harassing than the fear I was to experience two decades later of my never being able to bring my English prose anywhere close to the level of my Russian" (265).

This excerpt from Nabokov's autobiography provides a good description of the difficulty we encounter when we abandon our own language and also how this language, in time, turns into our only place of belonging. For this reason, we want to protect it from possible "foreign influences," because it is the only thing that still remains with us. At the same time, this *capsule*, to quote Brodsky, this refuge that is difficult to protect in a foreign land, carries within itself a world that we often discover while we are far away, or better, we discover that we belong to it only after leaving it.

A year after the publication of *Lolita*, Nabokov wrote an afterword: "On a Book Titled *Lolita*." In this essay, nowadays included in every edition of the novel, Nabokov tells of the trials and tribulations he encountered to publish it, and concludes with a reference to his "natural idiom" that he abandoned in 1940: "My private tragedy, which cannot, and indeed should not, be anybody's concern, is that I had to abandon my natural idiom, my untrammeled, rich and infinitely docile Russian tongue for a second-rate brand of English, devoid of any of those apparatuses—the baffling mirror, the black velvet backdrop, the implied associations and traditions—which the native illusionist, frac-tails flying, can magically use to transcend the heritage in his own way. (November 12, 1956)."[2]

During my first few years in Italy, I remember that my attachment to my mother tongue grew stronger than ever. I did not want to lose it and did everything in my power to safeguard it from any possible *contamination* or from any kind of weakening because, like it or not, distance severs ties, sometimes even our emotional ones, and along with them our connection to our language fades. When I traveled to Argentina, always for brief visits, I would return to Italy with boxes full of Spanish books, or I had friends and relatives mail them to me. For many years I read and wrote only in my mother tongue. Those sounds, those words carved inside of me the only refuge I had. They made it more spacious, more habitable, not minuscule and harsh as it appeared to me. I read Julio Cortázar, for instance, who had left Argentina in 1951 to go live in Paris and had continued to write in Spanish his whole life (he translated Poe, Defoe, Chesterton, and Yourcenar into Spanish and couldn't care less about his Parisian isolation).

Then, after my son's birth in 2000, I started writing a short story in Italian that turned into my first book published in this language *Restituiscimi il cappotto* (Return my coat). While writing in a new language, I realized I had lost all of my previous certainties. I had left aside the body that contained me to put on a phantom that evaded me in every direction. I questioned every sentence, every single word. Perhaps we feel an initial reticence, an inhibition, when we start writing in a language that is not our own. We distance ourselves in a way we never did before because that was our own language, and we were inside of it.

Now, on the other hand, when we use another language, we need to tiptoe in, making as little noise as possible. We scour the dictionary, we translate, we compare everything, until we find a word that creates an opening, a possibility. We lose many things when we switch languages, but we discover many others. Jhumpa Lahiri describes the difficulty of living in another language in her autobiographical text *In Other Words* in which she explains what this moment of transition from one language into another—in her case from English into Italian—means: "I lack the distance that would help me. I have only the distance that would hinder me. . . . But ultimately when I write I am in a trench."[3]

Living in another language also means writing on the margins, sometimes without being able to enter "the interior of the language . . . the subterranean parts" (92). With time, though, the veil is lifted and the hidden folds are revealed. In essence, we proceed, stumbling around, losing some pieces while finding some new ones that we might also lose because we do not always manage to hold them in our hands or in our pockets. We go forward in fits and starts.

Our relationship with the new language is, we might say, almost erotic. It is a relationship we constantly assess and revise, depending on how close we are to it. Julia Kristeva in *Strangers to Ourselves* reflects on a similar experience:

> Not speaking one's mother tongue. Living with resonances and reasoning that are cut off from the body's nocturnal memory, from the bittersweet slumber of childhood. Bearing within oneself like a secret vault, or like a handicapped child—cherished and useless—that language of the past that withers without ever leaving you. You improve your ability with another instrument, as one expresses oneself with algebra or the violin. You can become a virtuoso with this new device that moreover gives you a new body, just as artificial and sublimated— some say sublime. You have a feeling that the new language is a resurrection: new skin, new sex. But the illusion bursts when you hear, upon listening to a recording, for instance, that the melody of your voice comes back

to you as a peculiar sound, out of nowhere, closer to the old spluttering than to today's code.[4]

Our own mother tongue always returns under various maternal forms. Sometimes we distance ourselves from it to defend ourselves, or we get closer not to lose it. Switching languages presumes, in Nabokov's words, a "private tragedy." We experience transmigration, but without losing our past, because, in this case, the past is revisited in the light of a new language. At that point, we feel like our life is split, contested among two or more languages. And each memory speaks its own language.

~ 27 ~

# Language as a Line
# of Defense

American psychiatrist Ralph Greenson is famous for having
been Marilyn Monroe's analyst in the last months of her life
and also the analyst of many Vietnam veterans and of celeb-
rities such as Frank Sinatra and Tony Curtis. In a 1950 essay,
"The Mother Tongue and the Mother" later included in the
volume *Explorations in Psychoanalysis*, Greenson recounts his
clinical experience with an Austrian woman who had
emigrated to the United States as a young girl. After a few
sessions in English, Dr. Greenson invited the woman to
continue in German although she was fearful because she felt
that, in German, she would remember many things that she
wanted to keep buried forever. In German she saw herself as

a "scared, dirty child," in English, on the other hand, she described herself as "a nervous, refined woman."

Everything, even her relationships, had a different connotation for the Austrian woman, depending on the language. Analyzing this clinical case, Dr Greenson stated that the new language offered his patient "an opportunity to build up a new defensive system against her past infantile life" (38). It basically helped her to isolate and remove the Oedipal world she had created in German. The new language, therefore, gave her the possibility to remove or hide her memories. English was a sort of defense against her own mother tongue. Greenson explained that a new language provided the opportunity "for the establishment of a new self-portrait. This may supplant the old images" (39).

What this American psychiatrist was trying to demonstrate is that languages can either help us, or force us, to create a sort of split personality, so that we can be "a scared, dirty child" in German or "a nervous, refined woman" in English. This refuge from inner conflicts, this new language that takes over to mask or unveil was, Dr. Greenson explained, a way to keep, and at the same time, to sever the connection to the mother.

This topic is also explored in *The Babel of the Unconscious*, an interesting book because of its psychoanalytic dimension. It is also appreciated because it is an exploration of the mind of those who dream, think, and speak in more than one language. The authors write about the difficulty of looking at our traumatic experiences in the light of a new language: "We were able to understand how an analysand, by speaking about the conflicts and anxieties of his childhood in a second language learned in adulthood, could construct a kind of 'safety barrier' against the tumult of primitive emotions that would immediately have been evoked by the words of his mother tongue."[1]

To what extent, we can ask ourselves, does this "safety barrier" make us conscious of who we really are? How much does it reveal, and how much does it cover up? Is it then possible, I still wonder, to create another image of ourselves through a new language?

A dear friend of mine, Adelaida Gigli, was an extraordinary artist. Born in Italy in 1927, she and her parents emigrated to Argentina in 1930. Her father, the painter Lorenzo Gigli, had twice participated in the Venice Biennale at the height of fascism, but had later decided to leave Italy. For half a century, my friend had lived in Buenos Aires but in 1977 had chosen to go into exile, paradoxically, back to Recanati, the town of her birth. She was the mother of two children—*desaparecidos*—who disappeared during the military dictatorship: Maria Adelaida (nicknamed Mini) and Lorenzo Ismael. They were also the children of writer David Viñas with whom, in 1953, Adelaida had co-founded the literary journal *Contorno*. In an interview she declared that she had arrived back in Recanati "on the same day of my birth, but fifty years later."

I met her about ten years after her arrival in Italy. She lived in a colorful studio flat, where she preserved the memory of her children, filled with sculptures and paintings on the walls. There we used to read and talk late into the night (always with a bottle of whisky). Adelaida was a ceramist and a point of reference for Argentinian culture of the 1950s and 1960s.

I must admit that it was she, in that studio in Recanati, with a window facing the Cloister of Saint Augustine, who made me understand the many background stories behind Argentinian literature and allowed me to discover what it meant to be a Latin American. She spoke faltering Italian so most of the time the two of us spoke in Argentinian

Spanish. There were days though, or just moments, when she wanted to speak only Italian. I understood, or suspected, that in those moments there appeared in front of her the atrocious specter of that dictatorship that had taken her children, and she now needed to remove those inner voices through her newly acquired language. Adelaida lived between two languages and used them when needed to silence those inner demons that relentlessly stalked her. In the last years of her life she could no longer speak any language. Disease forced her into a long silence, and I do not know—I do not think anyone could—if those ghosts continued to torment her. It is difficult to struggle between two languages when one of them represents a world that caused such intolerable suffering. It would be equally difficult, though, to find ourselves unable to express in any language the pain for the loss of two children. Eventually, in the fall of 2010, Adelaida passed away, silently, in a hospice bed, with no language by her side.

A language, therefore, can be a defense against the past, it can forget or manipulate it, but it can also be a strategy (more or less conscious) to maintain a strong bond with our childhood. According to Brodsky who was well aware of the dilemma of dwelling in one's native language and then having to replace it, language is the *shield* or the *capsule* in which the foreigner seeks shelter. For Brodsky that capsule at some point after his exile, had turned into a prison, the space of an irreparable fracture.

During the first hearing of his trial held in Leningrad on February 8, 1964, while the regime accused him of pursuing a parasitic way of life (*tunejadstvo*), Brodsky clearly stated that he was a poet of the Russian language, and intended to remain so. Eight years later, on June 4, 1972, after being expelled from the Soviet Union, he sent a letter to Leonid

Brezhnev in which he reiterated his attachment to the Russian language. Brodsky considered language his only form of belonging to his country, which is why he wasn't afraid to denounce its corruption. Until 1976, the year he wrote his first essay in English, he had constantly experienced a sort of linguistic collision. Then, the change of language brought him to conceive of his adopted language, English, as a defense against Soviet totalitarianism. This is clear in the following excerpt about his American exile taken from his essay "Flight from Byzantium":

> I write this in English because I want to grant them [his family] a margin of freedom: . . . I want Maria Volpert and Alexander Brodsky to acquire reality under "a foreign code of conscience," I want English verbs of motion to describe their movements. This won't resurrect them, but English grammar may at least prove to be a better escape route from the chimneys of the state crematorium. . . . I know that one shouldn't equate the state with language but it was in Russian that two old people, shuffling through numerous state chancelleries and ministries in the hope of obtaining a permit to go abroad for a visit to see their only son before they died, were told repeatedly, for twelve years in a row, that the state considers such a visit "unpurposeful". . . . May English then house my dead. . . . For Maria Volpert and Alexander Brodsky, though, English offers a better semblance of afterlife, maybe the only one there is, save my very self. And as far as the latter is concerned, writing this in this language is like doing those dishes: it's therapeutic.[2]

English, not Russian, is the language that Brodsky hopes will house his parents in the afterlife. He uproots his father and mother from their mother tongue and houses them in a foreign language, because the new language can offer them a proper, more worthy burial. Brodsky buries his parents linguistically; he entrusts them to a language, English, that was also the maternal language of W. H. Auden whom he considered the greatest mind of the twentieth century. In fact, during an interview, Brodsky stated: "If asked to write prose in Russian I wouldn't be so keen. But in English it's a tremendous satisfaction. As I write I think about Auden, what he would say."[3]

But Brodsky writes in English also to give more dignity to his parents, to free them from the prison of their language. Writing his parents' names in English means, in fact, revisiting their story, removing it from corruption to give it new life in another grammar, another sound or a linguistic "elsewhere." In other words, a new voice that transforms that journey that Maria Volpert and Aleksander Brodsky were never allowed to undertake into a joyful welcome, more dignified than the one offered by the Russian chancelleries. I also wonder if my friend Adelaida Gigli would have done the same, had she been able to, for her children, Mini and Lorenzo Ismael. Switching languages is also useful for this, to find our freedom.

# ~ 28 ~

# The Maternity of
# Language II

At the heart of every language there exists a particular perspective and temporal structure. Each language conjugates the past, the present, and the future in its own way. Therefore, in some languages I can create sentences and grammatical constructions that in other languages would sound completely off key, even incomprehensible. Language is a way of seeing and of interpreting everything. It even shapes our behavior. We might even say that we are not born in, nor live in, a world, but rather in a language. That is why switching languages implies a different representation of reality. Yet, when we switch from one language to another, a part of that perspective that was contained in the first language still remains, like a hidden maternity. Behind the Italian that

I am using to write this book I hear the echo of a voice that is a combination of memories—remembered and forgotten—that belong to the Castilian Spanish of my childhood.

The new language grows superimposed on the seeds of our mother tongue. There is an inner dialogue, there are different roles that languages have inside of us, and fragments that survive anchored to a particular language and are difficult to uproot. We love in a language, we weep in another, we add up in the one we learned to count in and, above all, we hurl insults in the first language we learned, even if other languages might offer more colorful epithets.

Similarly, our mother tongue ("the cause of my being" according to Dante in the *Convivium*) develops on top of the seeds of a *primitive and pre-native* language that is babbled and echolalic, a repeated vocalization.[1] We carry this language inside of us and it is forever lost at the end of what Roman Jakobson defines as an infant's *apex of babble*: the passage from the pre-linguistic stage to the acquisition of the first words. In that precise moment of our existence, the shift is not gradual between the babbling—which contains limitless phonetic possibilities and therefore, potentially, all languages—and the articulation of our first word. On the contrary, it is a dramatic shift, a loss we can never redeem. It is there, in that abyss that separates babbling from the child's first spoken word that our first "forgetting" takes place in order to embark on our first radical passage from a pre-linguistic phase to the acquisition of our *mother tongue*. It is our first major jump into language. Daniel Heller-Roazen, in his intriguing book, *Echolalias: On the Forgetting of Language* asks himself if anything is left in adult language from the neonatal babbling: "Could it be that the child is so captivated by the reality of one language that he abandons the boundless but ultimately sterile realm that contains the possibility of all others? . . . is it the mother tongue that, taking hold of its new speaker, refuses to tolerate in him even the shadow of another?"[2]

Our mother tongue is born when our babbling stops, as Heller-Roazen explains: "It is as if the acquisition of language were possible only through an act of oblivion, a kind of linguistic infantile amnesia" (11). From this pre-linguistic stage we choose our mother tongue and forever forget our original language that potentially contained all the languages of the world. We can say that the key to language acquisition is in this act of forgetting. Therefore, the story of the Tower of Babel is repeated every time we as infants learn our mother tongue and forget the language that we started to articulate after birth. Without forgetting those sounds, those articulations, no language could be learned: "Perhaps the infant must forget the infinite series of sounds he once produced at the 'apex of babble' to obtain mastery of the finite system of consonants and vowels that characterizes a single language" (11).

Who knows if it is possible that something of that maternal Babel and babbling remains in us (Borges in one of his short essays claims that the English verb "to babble" and the German verb "babbeln" perhaps originated in the Tower of Babel and not from the first babbling of newborn infants). That "indistinct and immemorial babble that, in being lost, allowed all languages to be."[3] Learning a language presupposes this act of forgetting; it is our first experience and perhaps our first trauma. Going from one language to another, or from the original babbling to the mother tongue, means sacrificing a part of oneself: forgetting something to acquire something else. Dante refers to it as biblical confusion "that brought nothing else than oblivion to whatever language had existed before,"[4] and in Canto XXVI of *Paradiso* he has Adam express the following words: "The tongue I spoke was all extinct."

Perhaps in living we are destined to recover a lost and forgotten language. Learning to walk and talk means, therefore, leaving behind the magic world that contains our birth in order to begin to lose ourselves on earth. Our condition is similar to that of Baudelaire's albatross: exiled on earth, he is entangled on the deck of a ship, the sailors' prisoner, with his giant wings that prevent him from flying away. This gigantic bird, lord of the skies and of words, represents the tragedy of the fall, of a poet who no longer has his language, and is condemned to silence in a world that does not belong to him. We are inextricably bound to a language that contains us and imprisons us with its rules. Exiles, like Baudelaire's albatross, from that original language that had no rules and contained us in its boundlessness. And now we wander among languages, abandoned to eternal confusion, unable to recognize—or only with difficulty—the maternity that contains us in its silence. We are in transit among languages, and at the same time, transited by languages.

In 1902, Hugo von Hofmannsthal wrote a well-known piece: *Letter of Lord Chandos* in which Lord Chandos informs the recipient of the letter of his decision to give up writing and to choose silence, because he believed that no word, no language, was capable of expressing the reality of things. Therefore, he abandons writing and any possibility of dialogue. Lord Chandos has realized, following in the steps of others who have given up writing, that any language, no matter how precise, is inadequate to express the nature of things and of his own life. He understands that words are incapable of giving voice to things and therefore he claims his right to choose a language without words. Perhaps this imaginary character of Hofmannsthal's understands, more than anyone else, his condition of exile from a forgotten language he can no longer reclaim, when he states that "the language in which I might be able not only to write but to think is neither Latin nor English, neither Italian nor Spanish, but a language none of whose words is known to me, a language in which inanimate things speak to me and wherein I may one day have to justify myself before an unknown judge."[5]

# Notes

When no translator is indicated for non-English texts, the transaltion is ours.—Translators.

## Introduction

The Introduction and "The Difficulty of Abandoning One's Own Language" were previously published as "The New Language That Possesses Us." Paper presented at *Pluriverso italiano: incroci linguistico-culturali e percorsi migratori in lingua italiana*, Proceedings of the International Conference held at the University of Macerata, Macerata, Italy, and at the Recanati Campus, Recanati, Italy, December 10–11, 2015, ed. Carla Carotenuto, Edith Cognigni, Michela Meschini, and Francesca Vitrone (Macerata, Italy: M eum [Edizioni Università di Macerata], 2018), 705–713.

1. Joseph Brodsky, "To Please a Shadow," in *Less than One* (New York: Farrar, Straus & Giroux, 1983), 357.
2. Walter Benjamin, "The Storyteller: Reflections on the Works of Nicolai Leskov," in *Illuminations: Essays and Reflections*, ed. and intro. Hannah Arendt, trans. Harry Zohn (New York: Schocken, 1969), 92.

## Chapter 1    Childhood

**Note:** "Childhood" was previously published in slightly different form as "La maternità delle lingue," in *La Modernità Letteraria*, a journal edited by MOD (Società italiana per lo studio della modernità letteraria), issue titled *Immaginari migranti*, edited by Mario Domenichelli and Rosanna Morace.

## Chapter 2    Displacements

1. Rainer Maria Rilke, *Letters to a Young Poet* (Mineola, NY: Dover Publications, 2012), 12.
2. Gaston Bachelard, *La poétique de la rêverie* (Paris: Presses Universitaires de France, 1960), 104.
3. Antonio Prete, *Trattato della lontananza* (Turin: Bollati Boringhieri, 2008), 83.
4. Fernando Pessoa, *Poems of Fernando Pessoa*, trans. Edwin Honig and Susan M. Brown (San Francisco: City Lights Books, 1986), 97.

## Chapter 3    My Aunt's Languages

1. Ginevra Bompiani, "Il passato eventuale," in *Note di uno sconosciuto. Inediti e altri scritti*, ed. Antonio Delfini (Ascoli Piceno: Marka, 1990), 97.
2. Adrián Bravi, *Sud 1982* (Milan: Nottetempo, 2008), 108–109.
3. Przemysław Tacik, *The Freedom of Lights: Edmond Jabès and Jewish Philosophy of Modernity* (Bristol: Peter Lang, 2019), 319.
4. A few years ago, I already recounted my aunt's ocean crossing in my short story "Dopo la linea dell'Equatore" ("South of the Equator"). Adrián Bravi, *Variazioni Straniere* (Macerata: Eum Edizioni, 2015), 7–16.
5. Héctor Bianciotti, *Sans la miséricorde du Christ* (Paris: Gallimard, 1985), 42.

## Chapter 4   The Maternity of Language I

1. Silvia Baron Supervielle, *L'alphabet du feu petites études sur la langue* (Paris: Gallimard, 2007), 56.
2. Gaston Bachelard, *The Poetics of Reverie*, trans. Daniel Russell (Boston: Beacon Press, 1971), 32.
3. Dante Alighieri, *Il Convivio*, trans. Richard Lansing (New York: Garland, 1990).
4. Italo Calvino, *Hermit in Paris: Autobiographical Writings*, trans. Martin McLaughlin (Boston: Mariner Books, 2014), 172.
5. Joseph Brodsky, "The Condition we Call Exile," *The New York Review of Books*, January 21, 1988.

## Chapter 5   The Language of Love

1. Elias Canetti, *The Tongue Set Free: Remembrance of a European Childhood* (New York: Seabury Press, 1979), 27.
2. Anita Desai, *Notte e nebbia a Bombay* (Turin, Einaudi, 1999), VI–VII. Original English text unpublished, provided by Italian translator Anna Nadotti.
3. Hector Bianciotti, "Changing Language, Changing a Way of Being," accessed December 11, 2021, https://www .itinerariesofahummingbird.com/hector-bianciotti.html.
4. John Milton, *Poemata: Latin, Greek and Italian Poems by John Milton*, trans. William Cowper, last modified November 2004, https://ivu.org/history/renaissance/milton_poemata.htm.
5. Furio Brugnolo, *La lingua di cui si vanta Amore. Scrittori stranieri in lingua italiana dal Medioevo al Novecento* (Rome: Carocci, 2009), 78.
6. Milton, "Poemata."

## Chapter 6   The Hospitality of Language

1. Marcel Proust, *Against Sainte-Beuve and Other Essays*, trans. John Sturrock (London: Penguin, 1988), 93.

2. Gilles Deleuze and Claire Parnet, *Dialogues*, trans. Hugh Tomlinson and Barbara Habberjam (New York: Columbia University Press, 1987).

3. Herman Melville, "Bartleby, the Scrivener: A Story of Wall Street" SMK Books, 2013). Herman Melville, *Great Short Works of Herman Melville*. (Harper Perennial Modern Classics, 2004), 39–74.

4. Hugo von Hofmannsthal, *The Book of Friends*, trans. Douglas Robertson, accessed December 11, 2021, http://shirtysleeves .blogspot.com/2008/04/translation-of-buch-der-freunde-by -hugo.html.

## Chapter 7    The Enemy Language

1. Ágota Kristóf, *The Illiterate*, trans. Nina Bogin (London: CB Editions, 2014), 42.

## Chapter 8    The Possessiveness of Languages

1. Silvia Baron Supervielle, *L'alphabet du feu petites études sur la langue* (Paris: Gallimard, 2007), 55.

## Chapter 9    The Fluidity of Language

1. Luigi Meneghello, *Deliver Us,* trans. Frederika Randall (Evanston, IL: Northwestern University Press, 2011). Literal translation: *Deliver us from Malo/Evil* (*Malo*, Meneghello's hometown, is interpreted as related to the Latin word for *evil*, hence the title's pun on the Lord's Prayer: 'Deliver us from Malo/evil').

2. *Il Dispatrio* (The dispatriated) is a neologism with which Meneghello describes his condition of being an Italian intellectual living in England and how he is allowed to find his own national identity only by living abroad.

3. Meneghello, *Deliver Us*, 141–42.

4. Martin Heidegger, *On the Essence of Language,* trans. Wanda Torres Gregory and Yvonne Unna (Albany, NY: SUNY Press, 2004), 61.

5. Dolores Prato, *Giù la piazza non c'è nessuno,* edited by Giorgio Zampa (Macerata: Quodlibet, 2009), 219. Picador's Ravi Mirchandani and Farrar, Straus & Giroux's Jonathan Galassi and Jeremy Davies jointly acquired North American, UK, and Commonwealth English-language rights. Translation forthcoming, 2022.

6. Dolores Prato, *Le Ore II. Parole*, edited by Giorgio Zampa (Milan: Scheiwiller, 1988), 88.

7. Meneghello, *Deliver Us,* 337.

8. Jonathan Swift, *Gulliver's Travels* (Spain: Wordsworth Classics, 1992), 3. (Oxford University Press, 2008), 9.

## Chapter 10    Without Style

1. Samuel Knowlson, *Damned to Fame: The Life of Samuel Beckett* (New York: Grove Press, 2004), 156.

2. Israel Shenker, "Moody Man of Letters," *New York Times,* May 6, 1956, Sec. 2, p. 3.

3. Samuel Beckett, "Letter to Axel Kaun," in *Disjecta: Miscellaneous Writings and a Dramatic Fragment,* trans. Martin Esslin, ed. Ruby Cohn (London: John Calder, 1983), 171.

4. Nadia Fusini, "Beckett by Beckett," in *Samuel Beckett: Mal vu mal dit* (Turin: Einaudi, 1994), 89.

5. Deleuze and Parnet (1987), 4.

6. *On Grief and Reason: Essays by Brodsky, Joseph, 1940–1996* (NY: Farrar, Straus and Giroux, 1995), 30.

## Chapter 11    The Scent of the Panther

1. Dante Alighieri, *De Vulgari Eloquentia,* trans. Steven Botterill (Cambridge: Cambridge University Press, 1996).
2. Maria Corti, *Percorsi dell'invenzione. Il linguaggio poetico e Dante* (Turin: Einaudi, 1993), 76.
3. Dante Alighieri, *De Vulgari* I, 2, and 3.
4. Giorgio Agamben, "The Hunt for Language" in *The End of the Poem: Studies in Poetics*, trans. Daniel Heller-Roazen (Stanford: Stanford University Press, 1999), 141.
5. Giorgio Caproni, "Fragmentos de Khevenhüller," trans. Pedro Marqués De Armas, accessed December 11, 2021, https://rialta .org/giorgio-caproni-poemas/.

## Chapter 12    Prisoners of Our Own Language

1. Roland Barthes, *Writing Degree Zero,* trans. A. Lavers and Colin Smith (Boston: Beacon Press, 1967), 81.

## Chapter 13    Two Short Stories

1. Tommaso Landolfi, *Gogol's Wife and Other Stories*, trans. Rosenthal et al. (New York: New Directions Publishing, 1963), 30.
2. Dezső Kosztolányi, *Kornél Esti, A Novel,* trans. Bernard Adams (New York: New Directions Books, 2011).
3. Vladimir Jankélévitch, *Le Je-ne-sais-quoi et le presque-rien*, Vol. 2: *La Méconnaissance - Le Malentendu.* (Paris: Editions du Seuil, 1980).

## Chapter 15    Poetics of Chaos

1. Édouard Glissant, *An Introduction to a Poetics of Diversity* (Liverpool: Liverpool University Press, 2020), 24.

2. Anita Desai, *Notte e nebbia a Bombay* (Turin: Einaudi, 1999), vi–vii. Original English text unpublished, provided by Italian Translator Anna Nadotti.

3. Édouard Glissant, *Poetics of Relation*, trans. Betsy Wing (Ann Arbor: University of Michigan Press, 1997), 94.

4. Giacomo Leopardi, *Zibaldone*, trans. Baldwin et al. (New York: Farrar, Straus and Giroux, 2013), 202.

## Chapter 16  Exile

"Exile" was previously published in slightly different form as "Anche i pidocchi emigrano," *Prisma. Rivista dell'Ires Marche*, no. 2, 2010.

1. Friedrich Nietzsche, *Thus Spoke Zarathustra: A Book for Everyone and Nobody*, trans. Graham Parkes (Oxford: Oxford University Press, 2008), 13.

2. Victor Hugo, *La Légende des siècles* (English edition) (Scotts Valley, CA: CreateSpace Independent Publishing Platform, 2016).

3. Hugh of St Victor, *The Didascalicon* (New York: Columbia University Press, 1961), 101.

4. Tzvetan Todorov, *The Conquest of America: The Question of the Other* (New York: Harper & Row, 1985), 250.

5. Plutarch, "De Exilio," trans. Phillip H. De Lacy and Benedict Einarson, accessed December 11, 2021, http://penelope.uchicago .edu/Thayer/E/Roman/Texts/Plutarch/Moralia/De_exilio*.html.

## Chapter 17  Writing in Another Language

"Writing in Another Language" was previously published in slightly different form as "Narrare nella lingua migrante," in *Lingue migranti e nuovi paesaggi*, edited by Maria Vittoria Calvi, Irina Bajini, and Milin Bonomi (Dipartimento di Scienze della

Mediazione Linguistica e di Studi Interculturali, Università degli Studi di Milano), Milan, Edizioni universitarie di Lettere Economia Diritto (LED), 2015. A small part of "Writing in Another Language" was previously published in slightly different form as "Letteratura migrante," in *Piccolo Lessico del Grande Esodo. Ottanta lemmi per pensare la crisi migrante,* edited by Fabrice Olivier Dubosc and Nijmi Edres (Rome: Minimum Fax, 2017).

1. Rosanna Morace, *Un mare così ampio. I racconti-in-romanzo di Julio Monteiro Martins* (Rome: Libertà Edizioni, 2011), 33.

2. Raffaele Taddeo, *La lingua strappata. Testimonianze e letteratura migranti,* ed. Alberto Ibba and Raffaele Taddeo (Milan: Leoncavallo libri, 1999), 23.

3. Steven G. Kellman, *The Translingual Imagination* (Lincoln: University of Nebraska Press, 2000), x.

4. Rosanna Morace, *Letteratura-mondo italiana* (Pisa: Edizioni ETS, 2012), 10.

5. Melchíades is a character from *One Hundred Years of Solitude* by Gabriel García Márquez who is responsible for showing that there is an outside world.

## Chapter 19    Interference

1. Uriel Weinreich, *Languages in Contact: Findings and Problems* (Berlin: De Gruyter Mouton, 2010), 14.

2. Roberto J. Payró, "The Marriage of Laucha," trans. Anita Brenner, in *Tales from the Argentine,* ed. Waldo Frank (New York: Farrar & Rinehart 1930), 45–46.

## Chapter 20    Every Foreigner Is in Their Own Way a Translator

1. Julia Kristeva, *Intimate Revolt,* trans. Jeanine Herman (New York: Columbia University Press, 2002), 240.

## Chapter 21    Some Cases of Self-Translation

"Some Cases of Self-Translation" was previously published in slightly different form as "Casi di autotraduzione" in *Arcipelago Itaca*, no. 13, 2014, edited by Danilo Mandolini.

1. J. Rodolfo Wilcock, *Poesie spagnole* (Parma: Guanda, 1963), ix. Translations ours.

2. Wilcock, *Poesie spagnole*, xii–xiii.

3. Barth David Schwartz, ed., *Pasolini Requiem: Second Edition* (Chicago: University of Chicago Press, 2017), 123.

4. Witold Gombrowicz, *Diary*, Vol. 1 (1953–1958), trans. Lillian Vallee (Evanston, IL: Northwestern University Press, 1988), ix.

5. Ricardo Piglia, *Crítica y ficción* (Buenos Aires: Siglo veinte, 1993), 51.

6. Jacqueline Risset, "Joyce traduce Joyce," in *James Joyce, Scritti italiani* (Milan: Mondadori, 1979).

7. Nadia Fusini, "Beckett by Beckett," in Samuel Beckett, *Mal vu mal dit* (Turin: Einaudi, 1994), 88.

8. Derek Walcott, *What the Twilight Says: Essays* (New York: Farrar, Straus, and Giroux, 1998), 135–136.

9. Beckett, *Mal vu mal dit*, 88.

## Chapter 22    Identity and National Language

1. Translation partly taken from Sergio Waisman, *Borges and Translation* (Lewisburg, PA: Bucknell University Press, 2005), 24–25.

2. Silvia Baron Supervielle, *L'alphabet du feu petites études sur la langue* (Paris: Gallimard, 2007).

3. Beatriz Sarlo, *Escritos sobre literatura argentina* (Buenos Aires: Siglo ventiuno, 2007), 28.

## Chapter 23    The Language of Death

Parts of "The Abandonment of Language" and "The Language
of Death" were previously published in slightly different form as
"Quel che resta della lingua," in *Lingue migranti e nuovi paesaggi*,
edited by Maria Vittoria Calvi, Irina Bajini, and Milin Bonomi,
Dipartimento di Scienze della Mediazione Linguistica e di
Studi Interculturali, Università degli Studi di Milano (Milan:
Edizioni universitarie di Lettere Economia Diritto (LED),
2015).

1. Hannah Arendt, *The Last Interview and Other Conversations*
(New York: Melville House, 2013), 21–22.

2. Fred Uhlman, *Reunion* (London: Vintage Books, 2006), 79.

3. Anne Frank, *The Diary of a Young Girl*, trans. Susan Massotty
(New York: Knopf Doubleday Publishing Group, 2010), 67.

4. This and all remaining of Arendt's quotes are on pp. 22–23 of
*The Last Interview*.

5. Paul Celan, *Collected Prose*, trans. Rosemarie Waldrop (Hove,
UK: Psychology Press, 2003), 34.

6. Giorgio Agamben, *Idea of Prose*, trans. Michael Sullivan and
Sam Whitsitt (Albany: SUNY Press, 1995), 47.

7. Theodor W Adorno, "On the Question: 'What Is German?'" trans.
Thomas Y. Levin (*New German Critique* 36 (Autumn 1985): 121.

8. Jean Améry, *At the Mind's Limit: Contemplations by a Survivor
on Auschwitz and its Realities*, trans. Sidney Rosenfeld and
Stella P. Rosenfeld (Bloomington: Indiana University Press,
1980), 72.

9. Friedrich Nietzsche, "The Nietzsche Channel," accessed
December 11, 2021, http://www.thenietzschechannel.com/poetry
/poetry-dual.htm

10. Améry, *At the Mind's Limit*, 49–50.

## Chapter 24    Language as Property

1. Jacques Derrida, *Monolingualism of the Other OR The Prosthesis of Origin*, trans. Patrick Mensah (Palo Alto, CA: Stanford University Press, 1998), 25.


## Chapter 25    The Abandonment of Language

Parts of "Abandonment of Language" and "The Language of Death" were previously published in slightly different form as "Quel che resta della lingua," edited by Gianmaria Nerli, in *In pensiero. Arti e linguaggi del presente*, no. 9 (January–June 2015).

1. Claude Hagège, *On the Death and Life of Languages*, trans. Jody Gladding (New Haven: Yale University Press, 2009), 5.
2. Franz Rosenzweig, *The Star of Redemption*, trans. Barbara E. Galli (Madison: University of Wisconsin Press, 2005), 320.


## Chapter 26    The Difficulty of Abandoning One's Own Language

The Foreword and "The Difficulty of Abandoning One's Own Language" were previously published as "The New Language that Possesses Us," in *Pluriverso italiano: incroci linguistico-culturali e percorsi migratori in lingua italiana*, Proceedings of the International Conference held at the University of Macerata and at the Recanati Campus "L'infinito" on December 10–11, 2015. Edited by Carla Carotenuto, Edith Cognigni, Michela Meschini, Francesca Vitrone, 2018.

1. Vladimir Nabokov, *Speak, Memory: An Autobiography Revisited* (New York: G.P. Putnam's Sons, 1966), 265.
2. Vladimir Nabokov, *Lolita* (New York: Capricorn Books, 1972), 318–319.

3. Jhumpa Lahiri, *In Other Words*, trans. Ann Goldstein (New York: Knopf Doubleday Publishing Group, 2016), 9 and 93.

4. Julia Kristeva, *Strangers to Ourselves,* trans. Leon Roudiez. (New York: Columbia University Press, 1991.

## Chapter 27    Language as a Line of Defense

"Language as a Line of Defense" was previously published in slightly different form as "La lingua come difesa," in *Argentina 1976–1983: immaginari italiani*, edited by Camilla Cattarulla (Rome, Nuova Delphi, 2016).

1. J. Amati-Mehler, S. Argentieri, and J. Canestri, *The Babel of the Unconscious: Mother Tongue and Foreign Languages in the Psychoanalytic Dimension*, trans. Jill Whitelaw-Cucco (New York: International Universities Press, 1993), 2.

2. Joseph Brodsky, "Flight from Byzantium," in *Less than One: Selected Essays* (New York: Farrar, Straus, Giroux, 1986), 460–461.

3. Joseph Brodsky, interview by Sven Birkerts, December 1979, http://intelart.blogspot.com/2011/08/joseph-brodsky.html.

## Chapter 28    The Maternity of Language II

1. Dante Alighieri, *Il convivio*, trans. Richard Lansing, chapter 13, book 1.

2. Daniel Heller-Roazen, *Echolalias: On the Forgetting of Language* (New York: Zone Books, 2005), 11.

3. Heller-Roazen, 11–12.

4. Dante Alighieri, *De vulgari eloquentia*, trans. Steven Botterill (I, ix, 6).

5. Hugo von Hofmannsthal, "Letter of Lord Chandos," trans. Tania and James Stern, accessed December 11, 2021, http://www.jubilat.org/jubilat/archive/vol11/poem_10/.

# Bibliography

Adorno, Theodor W. "On the Question: 'What Is German?'"
    Translated by Thomas Y. Levin. *New German Critique*
    36 (Autumn 1985): 121–31.

Agamben, Giorgio. "The Hunt for Language." In *The End of the*
    *Poem: Studies in Poetics*, translated by Daniel Heller-Roazen.
    Stanford: Stanford University Press, 1999, 109–118.

———. *Idea of Prose.* Translated by Michael Sullivan and Sam
    Whitsitt. Albany: SUNY Press, 1995.

Alighieri, Dante. *Il convivio.* Translated by Richard Lansing.
    New York: Garland, 1990.

———. *De Vulgari Eloquentia.* Translated by Steven Botterill.
    Cambridge: Cambridge University Press, 1996.

Amati-Mehler, J., S. Argentieri, and J. Canestri. *The Babel of*
    *the Unconscious: Mother Tongue and Foreign Languages in the*
    *Psychoanalytic Dimension.* Translated by Jill Whitelaw-Cucco.
    New York: International Universities Press, 1993.

Améry, Jean. *At the Mind's Limit. Contemplations by a Survivor on*
    *Auschwitz and Its Realities.* Translated by Sidney Rosenfeld and
    Stella P. Rosenfeld. Bloomington: Indiana University Press, 1980.

Arendt, Hannah. *The Last Interview and Other Conversations.*
    New York: Melville House, 2013.

Bachelard, Gaston. *The Poetics of Reverie.* Translated by Daniel
    Russell. Boston: Beacon Press, 1971.

———. *La poétique de la rêverie.* Paris: Presses Universitaires de France, 1960.

Baron Supervielle, Silvia. *L'alphabet du feu petites études sur la langue.* Paris: Gallimard, 2007.

Barthes, Roland. *Writing Degree Zero.* Translated by Annette Lavers and Colin Smith. Boston: Beacon Press, 1967.

Beckett, Samuel. *Ill Seen, Ill Said.* London: John Calder, 1982.

———. "Letter to Axel Kaun." In *Disjecta: Miscellaneous Writings and a Dramatic Fragment.* Translated by Martin Esslin, edited by Ruby Cohn, 51-54.000–000. London: John Calder, 1983.

Benjamin, Walter. "The Storyteller: Reflections on the Works of Nicolai Leskov." In *Illuminations: Essays and Reflections.* Edited and introduced by Hannah Arendt, translated by Harry Zohn. New York: Schocken, 1969, 83–109.

Bianciotti, Hector. "Changing Language, Changing a Way of Being." Accessed December 11, 2021. https://www.itinerariesofahummingbird.com/hector-bianciotti.html.

———. *Sans la miséricorde du Christ.* Paris: Gallimard, 1985.

Bompiani, Ginevra "Il passato eventuale." In *Note di uno sconosciuto. Inediti e altri scritti.* Edited by Antonio Delfini, 97–102. Ascoli Piceno: Marka, 1990.

Bravi, Adrián. *Sud 1982.* Milan: Nottetempo, 2008.

Brodsky, Joseph. "The Condition We Call Exile." *The New York Review of Books*, January 21, 1988.

———. "Flight from Byzantium." In *Less than One: Selected Essays.* New York: Farrar, Straus, Giroux, 1986, 393–446.

———. Interview by Sven Birkerts. December 1979. http://intelart.blogspot.com/2011/08/joseph-brodsky.html.

———. *On Grief and Reason: Essays by Brodsky, Joseph, 1940–1996.* New York: Farrar, Straus and Giroux, 1995.

———. "To Please a Shadow," in *Less than One.* New York: Farrar, Straus & Giroux: 1983, 357–383.

Brugnolo, Furio. *La lingua di cui si vanta Amore. Scrittori stranieri in lingua italiana dal Medioevo al Novecento.* Rome: Carocci, 2009.

Calvino, Italo. *Hermit in Paris: Autobiographical Writings.* Translated by Martin McLaughlin. Boston: Mariner Books, 2014.

Canetti, Elias. *The Tongue Set Free: Remembrance of a European Childhood.* New York: Seabury Press, 1979.

Caproni, Giorgio. "Fragmentos de Khevenhüller." Translated into Spanish by Pedro Marqués De Armas. Accessed December 11, 2021. https://rialta.org/giorgio-caproni-poemas/.

Celan, Paul. *Collected Prose.* Translated by Rosemarie Waldrop. Hove, UK: Psychology Press, 2003.

Corti, Maria. *Percorsi dell'invenzione. Il linguaggio poetico e Dante.* Turin: Einaudi, 1993.

Deleuze, Gilles, and Claire Parnet. *Dialogues.* Translated by Hugh Tomlinson and Barbara Habberjam. New York: Columbia University Press, 1987.

Derrida, Jacques. *Monolingualism of the Other OR The Prosthesis of Origin.* Translated by Patrick Mensah. Palo Alto: Stanford University Press, 1998.

Desai, Anita. *Notte e nebbia a Bombay.* Turin: Einaudi, 1999.

Frank, Anne. *The Diary of a Young Girl.* New York: Knopf Double-day Publishing Group, 2010.

Fusini, Nadia. "Beckett by Beckett" In *Samuel Beckett: Mal vu mal dit.* Turin: Einaudi, 1994. 88.

Glissant, Édouard. *An Introduction to a Poetics of Diversity.* Liverpool: Liverpool University Press, 2020.

———. *Poetics of Relation.* Translated by Betsy Wing. Ann Arbor: University of Michigan Press, 1997.

Gombrowicz, Witold. *Diary.* Vol. 1 (1953–1958). Evanston, IL: Northwestern University Press, 1988.Hagège, Claude. *On the Death and Life of Languages.* New Haven: Yale University Press, 2009.

Heidegger, Martin. *On the Essence of Language.* Translated by
Wanda Torres Gregory and Yvonne Unna. Albany, NY: SUNY
Press, 2004.

Heller-Roazen, Daniel. *Echolalias: On the Forgetting of Language.*
Translated by Steven Botterill. New York: Zone Books, 2005.

Hofmannsthal, Hugo von. *The Book of Friends.* Translated by
Douglas Robertson. Accessed December 11, 2021. http://
shirtysleeves.blogspot.com/2008/04/translation-of-buch-der
-freunde-by-hugo.html.

———. "Letter of Lord Chandos." Translated by Tania and James
Stern. Accessed December 11, 2021. http://www.jubilat.org
/jubilat/archive/vol11/poem_10/.

Hugh of St Victor. *The Didascalicon.* New York: Columbia University
Press, 1961.

Hugo, Victor. *La Légende des siècles* (English Edition). Scotts Valley,
CA: CreateSpace Independent Publishing Platform, 2016.

Jankélévitch, Vladimir. *Le Je-ne-sais-quoi et le presque-rien,* Vol. 2:
*La Méconnaissance—Le Malentendu.* Paris: Editions du
Seuil, 1980.

Kellman, Steven G. *The Translingual Imagination.* Lincoln: University of Nebraska Press, 2000.

Knowlson, James. *Damned to Fame: The Life of Samuel Beckett.*
New York: Grove Press, 2004.

Kosztolányi, Dezső. *Kornél Esti, A Novel.* Translated by Bernard
Adams. New York: New Directions Books, 2011.

Kristeva, Julia. *Intimate Revolt.* Translated by Jeanine Herman.
New York: Columbia University Press, 2002.

———. *Strangers to Ourselves.* Translated by Leon Roudiez.
New York: Columbia University Press, 1991.

Kristóf, Ágota. *The Illiterate.* Translated by Nina Bogin. London:
CB Editions, 2014.

Lahiri, Jhumpa. *In Other Words.* Translated by Ann Goldstein.
New York: Knopf Doubleday Publishing Group, 2016.

Landolfi, Tommaso. *Gogol's Wife and Other Stories*. Translated by
Raymond Rosenthal, Jonathan Longrigg, and Wayland Young.
New York: New Directions Publishing, 1963.

Leopardi, Giacomo. *Zibaldone*. Translated by Kathleen Baldwin,
Richard Dixon, David Gibbons, Ann Goldstein, Gerard
Slowey, Martin Thom, and Pamela Williams. New York: Farrar,
Straus and Giroux, 2013.

Melville, Herman. "Bartleby, the Scrivener: A Story of Wall
Street." *Great Short Works of Herman Melville*. New York:
.Harper Perennial Modern Classics, 2004

Meneghello, Luigi. *Deliver Us*. Translated by Frederika Randall.
Evanston, IL: Northwestern University Press, 2011.

Milton, John. *Poemata: Latin, Greek and Italian Poems by John Milton*.
Translated by William Cowper. Last modified November, 2004.
https://ivu.org/history/renaissance/milton_poemata.htm.

Morace, Rosanna. *Letteratura-mondo italiana*. Pisa: Edizioni ETS, 2012.

———. *Un mare così ampio. I racconti-in-romanzo di Julio Monteiro
Martins*. Rome: Libertà Edizioni, 2011.

Nabokov, Vladimir. *Lolita*. New York: Capricorn Books, 1972.

———. *Speak, Memory: An Autobiography Revisited*. New York:
G.P. Putnam's Sons, 1966.

Nietzsche, Friedrich. "The Nietzsche Channel." Accessed December 11, 2021. http://www.thenietzschechannel.com/poetry/poetry
-dual.htm.

———. *Thus Spoke Zarathustra: A Book for Everyone and Nobody*.
Translated by Graham Parkes. Oxford: Oxford University
Press, 2008.

Payró, Roberto J. "The Marriage of Laucha." Translated by Anita
Brenner. In *Tales from the Argentine*. Edited by Waldo Frank.
New York: Farrar & Rinehart, 1930.

Pessoa, Fernando. *Poems of Fernando Pessoa*. Translated by
Edwin Honig and Susan M. Brown. San Francisco: City
Lights Books, 1986.

Piglia, Ricardo. *Crítica y ficción*. Buenos Aires: Siglo veinte, 1993.

Plutarch. "De Exilio." Translated by Phillip H. De Lacy and Benedict Einarson. Accessed December 11, 2021. http://penelope .uchicago.edu/Thayer/E/Roman/Texts/Plutarch/Moralia/De _exilio*.html.

Prato, Dolores. *Giù la piazza non c'è nessuno*. Edited by Giorgio Zampa. Macerata: Quodlibet, 2009.

———. *Le Ore II. Parole*. Edited by Giorgio Zampa. Milan: Scheiwiller, 1988.

Prete, Antonio. *Trattato della lontananza*. Turin: Bollati Boringhieri, 2008.

Proust, Marcel. *Against Sainte-Beuve and Other Essays*. Translated by John Sturrock. London: Penguin, 1988.

Rilke, Rainer Maria. *Letters to a Young Poet*. Mineola, NY: Dover publications, 2012.

Risset, Jacqueline. "Joyce traduce Joyce." In *James Joyce, Scritti italiani*. Milan: Mondadori, 1979, 197–214.

Rosenzweig, Franz. *The Star of Redemption*. Translated by Barbara E. Galli. Madison: University of Wisconsin Press, 2005.

Sarlo, Beatriz. *Escritos sobre literatura argentina*. Buenos Aires: Siglo ventiuno, 2007.

Schwartz, Barth David, ed.. *Pasolini Requiem*. 2nd. ed. Chicago: University of Chicago Press, 2017.

Shenker, Israel. "Moody Man of Letters." *New York Times*. May 6, 1956. Sec. 2, p. 3.

Swift, Jonathan. *Gulliver's Travels*. Oxford: Oxford University Press, 2008.

Tacik, Przemysław. *The Freedom of Lights: Edmond Jabès and Jewish Philosophy of Modernity*. Bristol: Peter Lang, 2019.

Taddeo, Raffaele. *La lingua strappata. Testimonianze e letteratura migrant*. Edited by Alberto Ibba and Raffaele Taddeo. Milan: Leoncavallo libri, 1999.

Todorov, Tzvetan. *The Conquest of America: The Question of the Other*. New York: Harper & Row, 1985.

Uhlman, Fred. *Reunion*. London: Vintage Books, 2006.

Waisman, Sergio. *Borges and Translation*. Lewisburg, PA: Bucknell University Press, 2005.

Walcott, Derek. *What the Twilight Says: Essays*. New York: Farrar, Straus, and Giroux, 1998.

Weinreich, Uriel. *Languages in Contact: Findings and Problems*. Berlin: De Gruyter Mouton, 2010.

Wilcock, J. Rodolfo. *Poesie spagnole*. Parma: Guanda, 1963.

# Notes on Contributors

ADRIÁN N. BRAVI, who is of Italian descent, was born in Argentina, where he spent the first twenty-four years of his life. He then settled in Italy, where he has lived for the last thirty-five years. Initially, he wrote only in Spanish, but once he began to write in Italian he wrote almost exclusively in his adopted language. His published work includes novels, essays, and short stories.

VICTORIA OFFREDI POLETTO (senior lecturer emerita) and GIOVANNA BELLESIA CONTUZZI (professor and chair) have taught and collaborated in the Department of Italian Studies at Smith College since 1990. They are committed to bringing the voices of migrant and second-generation women writers to the English-speaking world. Together they have translated many short stories from Italian into English as well as four other books: Genevieve Makaping's *Reversing the Gaze: What if the Other Were You?* (Rutgers University Press, 2023), Gabriella Ghermandi's *Queen of Flowers and Pearls*, Cristina Ali Farah's *Little Mother*, and Dacia Maraini's *Stowaway on Board*.